The Biblical Seminar
60

HISTORY AND IDEOLOGY

HISTORY AND IDEOLOGY

Introduction to Historiography in the Hebrew Bible

Yairah Amit

Translated by Yael Lotan

Sheffield Academic Press

Previously published as היסטוריה ואידיאולוגיה במקרא
(Tel Aviv: Ministry of Defence–The Publishing House, 1997)
Copyright © The Ministry of Defence, Israel

This first English language edition published
by Sheffield Academic Press Ltd
Mansion House
19 Kingfield Road
Sheffield S11 9AS
England

Copyright © 1999 Sheffield Academic Press

Printed on acid-free paper in Great Britain
by Cromwell Press
Trowbridge, Wiltshire

British Library Cataloguing in Publication Data

A catalogue record for this book is available
from the British Library

ISBN 1 85075 928 6

CONTENTS

PREFACE

This book is based on lectures I gave at Tel Aviv University on the subjects of history, narrative and ideology in biblical literature. The lectures were adapted as a series of 13 talks which I gave on the 'Broadcast University' of the Israeli Defence Forces Radio, sponsored by the Israeli Ministry of Defence and Tel Aviv University. This project arose from the idea that men and women while on their national service may wish to expand their general knowledge, and in addition to their military occupations seek access to the diverse subjects that are taught at the universities. Once a course has been broadcast, it is published as a book which serves as a key to further knowledge and interest in the subject. To date, there have been more than 300 courses on a variety of subjects, including the life sciences, the social sciences and others.

For this English edition I compiled talks that dealt with the same issue, so that it now contains ten chapters and an Afterword. Clearly such a narrow framework does not leave scope for a thorough study of this complex subject. However, the compression also offers advantages. For example, readers may gain a preliminary and, I hope, lucid idea of the subject, while the notes, together with the bibliography, can serve as a springboard for anyone who wishes to delve deeper.

I have chosen to use the new English translation of the Bible published by the JPS (Philadelphia: Jewish Publication Society of America, 1988), because of its modern language and more scholarly interpretation of the text, but I sympathize with those whose 'classical ear' is not happy with this choice.

Critical biblical research has always been somewhat iconoclastic. At the same time, taking my cue from Ecclesiastes that there is 'a time for tearing down and a time for building up' (3.3b), I have attempted to show that while denying the historicity of certain narratives, we move to a higher level, namely, their ideology. In other words, there is nothing nihilistic about my conclusion that many of the biblical stories do not reflect historical occurrences. On the contrary, it leads to an examination of the multifarious cultural developments the stories do reflect. Not only were these developments themselves part of history, but in the case of the Israelites, they also shaped the people for better or worse. In the words of the rabbis, 'The actions recounted of the patriarchs are indicative of what would later happen to their descendants', and we, the descendants, recapitulate the deeds of our forefathers—either foolishly and blindly, or observantly, soberly and sometimes painfully.

I wish to thank my friends Professor Nadav Na'aman, Professor Edward L. Greenstein and Professor Athalya Brenner, who read the manuscript. Their comments have helped me a great deal, though the final product reflects my own views. Special thanks are due to Professor David J.A. Clines of Sheffield Academic Press, who encouraged me to have the book translated, and to Yael Lotan who did the translation with knowledge and sensitivity. Last, but not least, to Rami, my life's companion, whose presence and support are the be all and end all.

ABBREVIATIONS

ANET	James B. Pritchard (ed.), *Ancient Near Eastern Texts Relating to the Old Testament* (Princeton, NJ: Princeton University Press, 1950)
ATANT	Abhandlungen zur Theologie des Alten und Neuen Testaments
BA	*Biblical Archaeologist*
BibB	Biblische Beiträge
BZAW	Beihefte zur *ZAW*
CBQ	*Catholic Biblical Quarterly*
FRLANT	Forschungen zur Religion und Literatur des Alten und Neuen Testaments
ICC	International Critical Commentary
JBL	*Journal of Biblical Literature*
JPS	Jewish Publication Society
JSOT	*Journal for the Study of the Old Testament*
JSOTSup	*Journal for the Study of the Old Testament*, Supplement Series
KJV	King James Version
KAT	Kommentar zum Alten Testament
LCL	Loeb Classical Library
NCBC	New Century Bible Commentary
OTL	Old Testament Library
PJ	*Palästina-Jahrbuch*
SBL	Society of Biblical Literature
SBLDS	SBL Dissertation Series
SBT	Studies in Biblical Theology
TZ	*Theologische Zeitschrift*
VT	*Vetus Testamentum*
VTSup	Vetus Testamentum, Supplements
WBC	World Biblical Commentary
WMANT	Wissenschaftliche Monographien zum Alten und Neuen Testament
ZAW	*Zeitschrift für die alttestamentliche Wissenschaft*

Chapter 1

THE IMPORTANCE OF HISTORY IN BIBLICAL LITERATURE

Interest in the past and the writing of history are prominent features of
biblical literature, a great part of which consists of a methodical narrative of sequential historical events.

The reader who opens the book of Genesis finds that it barely lingers
over the mythical period, during which the world was not as we know
it. Indeed, once Adam and Eve are expelled from the Garden of Eden
(Gen. 3), the historical era begins and the reader is presented with a
condensed chronicle of humanity, its achievements and above all its
failures, up to the advent of Abraham on the stage of history (Gen. 4–
11). Thereafter the historical narrative focuses on Abraham and his pos-
terity, and the reader learns about the patriarchal family that grew into a
clan (Gen. 12–36), and its migration to Egypt (Gen. 37–50), where it
increased and became a nation (Exod. 1.1-7). The narrative deals predominantly with the major events in the life of this nation, namely: the
Egyptian bondage, the Exodus from Egypt and the wanderings in the
wilderness (Exod. 1.8 to Deut. 34); the incomplete conquest of the
Promised Land (Joshua), and the time of the Judges, when the Israelites
were tempted to worship the gods of the surrounding peoples, were
punished, and consequently decided that they needed a king (Judg. 1 to
1 Sam. 8); finally, the reader is told about the establishment of the
monarchy and the splitting of the kingdom, followed by the chronicles
of the kingdoms of Judah and Israel until their downfall (from 1 Sam. 9
to 2 Kgs 25).

However, this historical sequence, which opens in the book of Genesis and concludes at the end of 2 Kings, is not all there is of biblical historiography. Special events are also described in the prophetic
books of the 'writing prophets'—that is, the classical prophets, such as
Amos, Isaiah and Jeremiah. Some events are described twice, both in
the book of Kings and by the Latter Prophets. For example, the siege of
Sennacherib and the treaty with Babylon in the reign of Hezekiah are

described in 2 Kings 18–20 and in Isaiah 36–39. Likewise, the fall of the kingdom of Judah is described at the end of 2 Kings (ch. 25), as well as at the end of Jeremiah (ch. 52). Of special interest are the references to events which appear only in the books of the Latter Prophets—for example, the joint attempt by Pekah (son of Remaliah, King of Israel) and Rezin (King of Aram) to conquer Judah and replace its King Ahaz with one called the son of Tabeal. This event is described only in Isa. 7.1-9. Similarly, the freeing of the slaves and their renewed enslavement, which took place in Jeremiah's time during Zedekiah's reign, is described only in Jeremiah 34.

Historical narrative also plays an important part in the books of the Writings, representing a later stage in the development of biblical literature, some of which depicts the early days of the Second Temple period. Thus the books of Ezra and Nehemiah describe the Babylonian exiles' return to Zion, and the book of Esther describes the persecution of the Jews and their deliverance in the reign of Ahasuerus, King of Persia. However, some of the historical books of the Writings hark back to earlier periods that were chronicled in previous books. The book of Ruth, for example, relates what appears to be a family story from the time of the Judges, namely, the marriage of Ruth and Boaz (the great-grandparents of David, foremost of the Israelite kings). Another example is the book of Chronicles, which spans a greatly extended period. After delineating in a condensed manner, using genealogical lists, the historical sequence from Adam to the reign of King Saul (1 Chron. 1–9), it slows down and describes in some detail the history of Israel under the rule of the House of David, from the death of Saul to the proclamation of Cyrus to the Babylonian exiles (1 Chron. 10–2 Chron. 36).

But the list of texts dealing with historical events would be incomplete without mentioning the liturgical book of Psalms, of which some chapters may be called historical psalms, as they describe significant events in the history of the nation. Two examples will suffice: Psalm 114, which opens with the words 'When Israel went forth from Egypt, the House of Jacob from a people of strange speech' (v. 1), and Psalm 137, which mentions the Babylonian conquest and opens with the words, 'By the rivers of Babylon, there we sat, sat and wept, as we thought of Zion' (v. 1).

For sheer quantity, then, the genre of historiography represents a large portion of biblical literature, and thereby acquires qualitative importance.

Some may question if indeed all the books and narratives I have mentioned qualify as historiography. Can the story of the wanderings in the wilderness, with all its miracles, be labelled historical writing? Or can the book of Chronicles, with its doubtful reliability and obvious bias, be described as a work of historiography? The doubt stems from accepted assumptions which were developed in Greek historiography, notably by Thucydides, the Greek historian of the fifth century BCE. His method rested on the belief that the writer of history must seek historical truth. A historian should use only reliable testimonies, avoid supernatural explanations based on miracles and divine intervention, and strive for objective descriptions.[1] Clearly, applying these criteria to the biblical chronicles of past events would undermine their historiographic character and value, and assign them to a different category. Today, however, under the influence of rationalist and sceptical currents, even historians have become persuaded that it is not possible to achieve a perfect truth, or to write a history which reflects objective truth. As the English historian Sir George Clark put it: 'Since all historical judgements involve persons and points of view, one is as good as another and there is no "objective" historical truth'.[2] Applying this conclusion to biblical history, we find that many of its narratives of past events would qualify as historiographic descriptions.

In other words, to question the application of the label 'historiography' to certain books or certain descriptions in the Bible because they are not sufficiently reliable or objective, or because they allow for miracles and divine intervention, is to overlook the intention of the authors to write history from their own standpoint and in accordance with their world-view. Whether or not this is reliable history is another question, which must be tackled with the tools of the science of history.[3] The biblical historians may therefore be compared to the writers of Marxist, feminist or some other 'official' history which reflects a particular ideology. In all these cases it is necessary to distinguish between the desire to present a historical description and the reliability

1.   Thucydides 1.21-22, cited in C.F. Smith (trans.), *Thucydides* (LCL; Cambridge, MA: Harvard University Press; London: Heinemann, 1956), pp. 37-41.

2.   Quoted in E.H. Carr, *What is History?* (Harmondsworth: Penguin Books, 1961), p. 8.

3.   On these problems see also R.G. Collingwood, *The Idea of History* (Oxford: Oxford University Press, 1946); A.D. Momigliano, *Studies in Historiography* (London: Weidenfeld & Nicolson, 1966).

of the finished product. We may therefore conclude that to qualify as
a historiographic work it is only necessary for the author to be con-
sciously seeking to describe the past. Whether or not it belongs to this
specific genre is determined neither by its historical reliablity nor by the
degree of its objectivity. No wonder, then, that when Josephus Flavius
set out to write a history of the Jews, he saw fit to rewrite every single
one of the biblical books referred to above. He incorporated the Pentateuch and the Former Prophets, the books of Ruth and Esther, Ezra,
Nehemiah and Chronicles, into those chapters that covered the biblical
era.[4]

So much for the preponderance of historiography in biblical literature, and its qualification as such. Indeed, the existence of so many such
writings testifies to the centrality of history, and of the historical awareness of the authors in shaping biblical literature. But the quantitative
observation is not all the evidence there is.

The significance of history in the minds of the biblical authors is also
evident in their efforts to provide a historical background for their various writings. Indeed, there are only a few stories in the Bible that lack a
historical setting; for example, like the book of Job, which opens with
the words: 'There was a man in the Land of Uz...' (Job 1.1). The
period in which he lived is not specified, and perhaps this was one of
the reasons that the Sages concluded that Job was not a historical figure: 'Job never was, he was only a parable' (*b. B. Bat.* 14b). But in
most cases the reverse is true—the historical setting is given at once,
and in many cases the openings of prophecies, hymns and books of
wisdom (Proverbs and Ecclesiastes) also refer to the period in which
they were composed, or in which the narrated events took place. Even
if we regard the reference to Koheleth the son of David, who was king
in Jerusalem, as unreliable because there are no data about a son of
David by that name,[5] it remains a detail that the book's editor saw fit to

---

4.   Josephus, *Ant.* 1–4 (see *Jewish Antiquities*, IV [trans. H.St.J. Thackeray;
LCL; Cambridge, MA: Harvard University Press; London: Heinemann, 1957]);
Ant. 5–8 (see *Jewish Antiquities*, V [trans. H.St.J Thackeray and R. Marcus; LCL;
Cambridge, MA: Harvard University Press; London: Heinemann, 1958]); *Ant.* 9–11
(see *Jewish Antiquities*, VI [trans. R. Marcus; LCL; Cambridge, MA: Harvard Uni-
versity Press; London: Heinemann, 1958]).

5.   For the lists of David's sons see 2 Sam. 3.2-5; 5.14-16; 1 Chron. 3.1-9; and
see also 1 Chron. 14.4-7. It is not surprising that the Sages, in the wake of Eccl.
1.12, identified Koheleth with Solomon; see *b. B. Bat.* 14b; *Cant. R.* 1.10.

state, thereby setting the text in a time and place and providing it with a historical background.[6]

The awareness of the importance of history is attested in another way. Most of the Hebrew editions of the biblical canon conclude with the books of Ezra, Nehemiah and Chronicles. The Babylonian Talmud has already laid down (in *B. Bat.* 14b) the order of the Writings, concluding with Ezra and Chronicles.[7] This finale provides the Hebrew Bible with a historical framework whose last boundary is the beginning of the Second Temple period. We recall that Chronicles concludes with the proclamation of Cyrus (2 Chron. 36.22-23). It does not matter if this was the original ending or was appended by the last editors of the biblical assemblage.[8] To us, the significant fact is that someone made a point of concluding the Bible with an event dated to the early days of Persian domination. This was, of course, the time of the last prophets— Haggai, Zechariah and Malachi—whom the tradition of the Sages associated with the ending of prophecy. This historical reference meant that the process of biblical composition came to an end at the same time as the phenomenon of prophecy: 'The rabbis have taught that with the death of the last prophets, Haggai, Zechariah and Malachi, prophecy was gone from Israel' (*b. Sanh.* 11a).[9] In other words, the historical framework of the complete body of biblical literature supports the claim that it was given in the spirit of prophecy and is therefore sacred.

6.   By the sixteenth century, Luther had already rejected the identification of Koheleth with Solomon. 'There is general consensus among critical scholars that the language and thought of the book point to the post-exilic period', R.E. Murphy, *Ecclesiastes* (WBC, 23A; Dallas: Word Books, 1992), p. xxii.

7.   The LXX has a different order of books. There the books of the law and the historiography precede the books of prophecy and poetry. Thus the book of Ruth is the continuation of Judges, and Chronicles, together with Ezra and Nehemiah, is located after Samuel and Kings.

8.   According to E.L. Curtis and A.L. Madsen (*The Books of Chronicles* [ICC; New York: Charles Scribner's Sons, 1910], p. 525) these verses show that at some previous stage Ezra, Nehemiah and Chronicles were one book. But S. Japhet (*I & II Chronicles* [OTL; Louisville, KY: Westminster/John Knox Press, 1993], pp. 1061-77) stresses that this ending characterizes both the aim and the poetics of the book, which means that it is an integral part of it.

9.   On the different versions of this saying and its purpose see E.A. Urbach, 'When Did Prophecy Cease?' (Heb.), *Tarbiz* 17 (1946), pp. 1-11.

The centrality of history in the composition and editing of the biblical complex is reflected not only in the plethora of historical descriptions and references, but also in the careful provision of historical backgrounds, and the sophisticated use of historical frameworks and contexts. All this testifies not only to the writers' awareness of history, but also to their aim of cultivating such awareness in their readers.

It should be noted that such a great interest in history is not universal, as Yerushalmi pointed out in the Foreword to his book *Zakhor*:

> For those reared and educated in the modern West it is often hard to grasp the fact that a concern with history, let alone the writing of history, is not an innate endowment of human civilization. Many cultures—past and present—have found no particular virtue in the historical, temporal dimension of human existence.[10]

Given this fact, we ought to ask what has caused the profound interest in history that is manifested in biblical literature. The answer to this question must be sought in the distinctive character of biblical monotheistic religion.[11]

The concept of divinity as developed in biblical literature is of a single universal deity who manifests himself in history, conducts a continuous dialogue, direct or indirect, with humankind, and is not only a cosmic divinity in command of nature, but also a kind of providence, supervising human history and directing it. This concept gave rise to a new attitude to history, which came to replace mythology. Reducing the pantheon of many gods to a single one meant discarding the stories of their deeds and replacing them with a description of the relations between the one God and humankind, his creatures. God is thus displaced from the world of myth, which moves along eternal time cycles, and interest becomes focused on the connection between him and humanity, thus giving a new significance to human events. These, in turn, become means of learning and understanding God's ways.

10. Y.H. Yerushalmi, *Zakhor: Jewish History and Jewish Memory* (Seattle: University of Washington Press, 1982), p. 6.

11. As to the term 'biblical religion', I accept the view of S.A. Geller (*Sacred Enigmas: Literary Religion in the Hebrew Bible* [London: Routledge, 1996]) that the biblical texts represent a variety of religious views, and that this term is essentially pluralistic. He uses this term because of scholarly tradition and for convenience.

It is therefore not surprising that as biblical religion developed, history became one of its essential constituents, as the basis for God's expectations of and demands on his people.

Various laws took on historical justification. Thus, for instance, in Deut. 15.15, the injunction to give the freed Hebrew slave a liberal gift and not 'let him go empty-handed', is justified as follows: 'Bear in mind that you were slaves in the land of Egypt and the Lord your God redeemed you; therefore I enjoin this commandment upon you today'. The same reasoning appears in connection with the observance of the Sabbath in the Deuteronomic version of the Ten Commandments (Deut. 5.14-15), and in some other laws too. In some cases it is possible to follow the gradual process, as for example in reference to the three annual feasts. In the Book of the Covenant the three feasts are mainly linked to the seasons and agricultural life: the feast of unleavened bread[12] in the spring; the feast of the early crop harvest in the time of the first fruits; and the feast of ingathering at the end of the year (Exod. 23.14-17). These festivals gradually became more linked with past events and detached from their original association with nature.[13] In Deuteronomy, Passover and the Feast of unleavened bread are linked to the Exodus from Egypt with repeated explanations (16.1-8), and Leviticus continues the process with regard to the feast of Tabernacles, stating that the children of Israel lived in booths when they came out of Egypt (Lev. 23.42-43);[14] whereas the association of the feast of Pentecost with the giving of the Law was made later still, and may be found in the apocryphal texts and the tradition of the Sages.[15]

---

12. Only in the case of the feast of unleavened bread is the historical context mentioned, and then only in a very short way: 'For in it you went forth from Egypt' (Exod. 23.15). Critical scholars are convinced that it is a later addition. See, e.g., M. Noth, *Exodus* (OTL; trans. J.S. Bowden; London: SCM Press, 2nd edn, 1966), p. 191; J.P. Hyatt, *Exodus* (NCBC; Grand Rapids: Eerdmans, 1980), p. 248; and elsewhere.

13. Cf. J. Wellhausen, *Prolegomena to the History of Ancient Israel* (trans. J.S. Black and A. Menzies; New York: Meridian Books, 2nd edn, 1958 [1878]), pp. 83-120.

14. The calendar of feasts in Lev. 23 is part of the Book of Holiness, which is the last layer of the Pentateuch. On the late date of the School of Holiness see I. Knohl, *The Sanctuary of Silence: The Priestly Torah and the Holiness School* (Minneapolis: Fortress Press, 1995). His main argument is based on the analysis and comparison of the feasts' calendars in Lev. 23 and Num. 28–29.

15. See *Jub.* 1.1; 6.17-22; 15.1-2; *Mek.*, Jethro; *b. Šab.* 86b-87a and parallels.

Even the way God represents himself is linked to a historical context. When God appeared to Moses in the burning bush he introduced himself as the God of the forefathers (Exod. 3.6). Later, when he appeared to the entire people on Mount Sinai, he said: 'I the Lord am your God who brought you out of the land of Egypt, the house of bondage' (Exod. 20.2). As Ibn-Ezra noted and asked in the name of Rabbi Yehuda Halevy: 'Why did He say "I the Lord am your God who brought you out of the land of Egypt", rather than "I the Lord am your God who created heaven and earth and made you"?'

Finally, the role of history in biblical literature is not limited to historical descriptions and contexts; it is also explicit in the injunction to recall and repeat the events of the past in connection with various rites and objects. Thus, for example, the setting of the 12 stones in Gilgal, after the crossing of the Jordan, is explained as prompting a retelling of history: 'In time to come, when your children ask their fathers, "What is the meaning of those stones?", tell your children: "Here the Israelites crossed the Jordan on dry land". For the Lord your God dried up the waters of the Jordan before you until you crossed, just as the Lord your God did to the Sea of Reeds, which He dried up before us until we crossed...' (Josh. 4.21-24; cf. vv. 6-7).

The retelling of history in conjunction with rituals has the advantage of being cyclic and permanent, as in the injunction to tell the story of the Exodus from Egypt every year while celebrating the feast of unleavened bread: 'And you shall explain to your son on that day, "It is because of what the Lord did for me when I went free from Egypt" ...You shall keep this institution at its set time from year to year' (Exod. 13.8-10).[16]

A broader historical canvas, ranging from the time of the forefathers to the Exodus and the conquest of Canaan, is recapitulated in the rite of bringing the first fruits to the priest in the temple. The bringer of the first fruits narrates the history from 'My father was a fugitive Aramaean. He went down to Egypt with meagre numbers...' up to 'and gave us this land, a land flowing with milk and honey' (Deut. 26.5-9).

A paean to the telling of history and its transmission from generation to generation also appears in the opening of Psalm 78, praising the 'things we have heard and known, that our fathers have told us. We will

---

16. See also vv. 11-16 and 12.26-27; cf. *m. Pes.* 10.5: 'In every generation each individual is bound to regard himself as if he personally had gone forth from Egypt, as is said...'

not withhold them from their children, telling the coming generation the praises of the Lord and his might, and the wonders He performed'. And the purpose of all this is that they will not 'forget God's great deeds, but observe His commandments...' (Ps. 78.1-8).

These examples, among many others, support the enthusiastic conclusion of the English historian Herbert Butterfield in the entry 'Historiography', which he wrote for the *Encyclopaedia Hebraica*: 'The general outcome was that they were almost obsessed with history, and they worshipped God more as the lord and ruler of history than as the creator of the world...Never in ancient times did history attain such prominence.'[17]

To sum up, when biblical literature harks back to the past it is apparently to the historical rather than the mythical past; to the time when, in the words of Yerushalmi, 'the great and critical moments of Israel's history were fulfilled. Far from attempting a flight from history, biblical religion allows itself to be saturated by it, and is inconceivable apart from it'.[18]

But, if history was so important, we should ask when it began to be written. The next chapter deals with this question.

17. H. Butterfield , 'Historiography', *Encyclopaedia Hebraica*, XIV (Jerusalem and Tel Aviv: Encyclopaedia Publishing Company, 1960; Heb.), pp. 259-318 (264).
18. Yerushalmi, *Zakhor*, p. 9.

Chapter 2

WHEN DID THEY START WRITING HISTORY?

Let me begin by stating that there is still widespread disagreement among scholars with regard to the sensitive question as to when biblical history began to be written. But before outlining the main opinions on this issue let me clarify the distinction between chronicles, which have been generally known since time immemorial, and historiographical works, such as the biblical one.

Chronicles are historical compositions that record events, dryly and matter-of-factly, in the order in which they occur. This category includes brief descriptions of events, one by one, as a series of acts associated with a particular central subject, or a selection of occurrences in the order in which they took place. Much of the data in these chronicles lacks interior causality. By contrast, historiography links its data in a causal chain of events, creating a continuous historical composition. Historiography is a description of the past that outlines its operating factors, the chain of events and their outcome, based on causal principles. This type of writing makes use of various historical sources, possibly including chronicles, in its quest to understand the past, its mysteries and its rules. The distinction between history writing and chronicles is emphasized by Walsh:

> The historical ideal is always to get away from the stage of chronicle and attain that of history itself. What every historian seeks for is not a bare recital of unconnected facts, but a smooth narrative, in which every event falls as it were into its natural place and belongs to an intelligible whole.[1]

To illustrate the difference between chronicle and historiography, here is an excerpt from the Abingdon Chronicle, part of the Anglo-

---

1.   W.H. Walsh, *An Introduction to Philosophy of History* (London: Hutchinson, 3rd edn, 1967 [1951]), p. 34.

Saxon Chronicle, written in a mediaeval English monastery and covering the years 1044–1046:[2]

> 1044—In this year Archbishop Eadsige resigned from his bishopric because of ill health...In this year there was a very great famine over England, and corn was dearer than anyone remembered, so that the 'sester' of wheat rose in price to sixty pence and even higher. This same year the King sailed out to Sandwich with thirty-five ships...In this same year King Edward took to wife Edith, the daughter of Earl Godwine, ten days before Candlemas.

> 1045—In this year the Bishop Beorhtwold passed away on 22 April... In the summer of this same year King Edward sailed out with his ships to Sandwich; and so large a host was gathered there that no man had ever seen a greater naval force in this land...

> 1046—In this year the Earl of Swein marched into Wales...When he was on his homeward way, he had the abbess of Leominster fetched to him, and kept her as long as he pleased, and then let her go home...After Candlemas in this same year came the severe winter with frost and snow and widespread storms; it was so severe that no living man could remember another like it...

It is plain to see that this chronicle records important facts side by side with anecdotes and trivia.

Another example, closer to the period and culture under discussion, is taken from a Babylonian chronicle from the first years—fourth to eighth—of the reign of Nebuchadnezzar, king of Babylon (601–597 BCE). The record of the seventh year is of special interest, as it refers to the conquest of Jerusalem in the reign of Jehoiachin (598 BCE), the exiling of the king and his replacement with Zedekiah:

> Year Four—The king of Akkad mustered his army and set out for the land of Hatti. In Hatti he moved about as ruler. In the month of Kislev he headed his army and marched on Egypt. The king of Egypt heard and mustered his army. Confronting each other in the open field, they fought and inflicted heavy losses upon each other. The king of Akkad and his army turned back [to go] to Babylon.

> Year Five—The king of Babylon in his land. He organized his chariots and his many horses.

---

2. I am following E. Weinryb, *Historical Thinking: Issues in Philosophy of History* (Tel-Aviv: Everyman's University Publishing House, 1987; Heb.), pp. 19-20. The quote is taken from G.N. Garmonsway (ed. and trans.), *The Anglo-Saxon Chronicle* (London: J.M. Dent, 1972), pp. 163-65.

Year Six—In the month of Kislev the king of Akkad mustered his army and set out for the land of Hatti. From Hatti he sent forth his army which raided the desert and captured much of the property, cattle and tents of the many sons of Arabia. In the month of Adar the king returned to his country.

Year Seven—In the month of Kislev the king of Akkad mustered his army and set out for the land of Hatti. He besieged the city of Judah (URU Ia-a-hu-du), and on the second day of Adar conquered the city and captured its king. He set a king of his choice on the throne. He t[ook] its rich tribute and carried it away to Babylon.

Year Eight—In the month of Tevet the king of Akkad [set out] for the land of Hatti, reaching as far as Carchemi[sh…] and in the month of Shevat the king returned to his country.[3]

Chronicles were typically written soon after the events they described. The chronicler generally put down the occurrences in the order in which they took place, without seeking the connections between them or sifting the significant from the trivial, and without regard for the aesthetic or rhetorical qualities of his representation. By contrast, the historian usually writes long after the events and learns about the past from such sources as the chronicles. As a result, he has indirect knowledge of past events and views them from a historical perspective. Above all, he seeks to understand the causes of the events he has chosen to describe, and how they are linked together. Not all the actions of the king are of interest to him, only those which affect the development of events with reference to the forces that operate in history, such as economics, international relations, domestic policies, and so on. At the same time, he attempts to present his material in an interesting and convincing manner so as to captivate his readers.

While chronicles are known from the Hittite, Egyptian and Mesopotamian cultures, the only known continuous and systematic historical composition from the ancient Near East is the Israelite one. Greek and Roman historiography was written some time later.

The biblical-historical writings refer to the various sources that were available to the authors. Among them was the 'Book of Jashar', which described how the sun and the moon came to the aid of Joshua: 'Stand still, O sun, at Gibeon, O moon, in the Valley of Aijalon! And the sun stood still and the moon halted, while a nation wreaked judgment on its

---

3.   I am indebted to Professor Nadav Na'aman for the use of his translation.

foes—as is written in the Book of Jashar' (Josh. 10.12-13). It also contained the lament of David for Saul and Jonathan (2 Sam. 1.18). Other sources were the 'Book of the Wars of the Lord' (Num. 21.14), the 'Book of the Annals of Solomon' (1 Kgs 11.41), the 'Annals of the Kings of Judah' (1 Kgs 14.29, and elsewhere) and the 'Annals of the Kings of Israel' (1 Kgs 14.19 and elsewhere). And indeed, the historical books that state explicitly that they made use of these sources—for example—the book of Joshua or the book of Kings—are concerned with the factors that affected the life of the people, draw conclusions about the laws of history, and as written narratives are naturally meant to serve as lessons for future generations. We must therefore focus on the question as to when historical books such as Joshua and Kings were written, as distinct from their sources.

It should be noted, however, that the beginning of historiography is usually attributed to Herodotus, a Greek historian whose work was already known in the latter half of the fifth century BCE, and who is called 'the father of history'.[4] The reason for this is chiefly the breadth of his composition and his perception of events as parts of an extensive and comprehensive system. But Herodotus did not manifest a desire to get at the truth any more than did the biblical narratives, nor did he seek to analyse and evaluate his sources; he too relied on popular traditions and theological explanations of events, which included the gods and could be categorized as miracles. Recognizing that no historical writing fully reflects truth and objectivity—as noted in Chapter 1—and that the historical texts in the Bible have a breadth of chronological sequence and a perception of Israel's place among the nations, I am led to conclude that the biblical descriptions of the past qualify as historiography, and that the beginning of historiography may therefore be ascribed to Israel, earlier still than Herodotus's work. We must now ask how long before Herodotus was the beginning of historiography and when biblical history began to be written down.

In an article entitled 'The Rise of Historiography in Israel', published in the early 1950s, Cassuto upheld the view which was first propounded in the nineteenth century and is still accepted by many scholars, that the writing of history began in Israel in the tenth century BCE, namely, 'in

---

4. A.D. Godley (trans.), *Herodotus: In Four Volumes* (LCL; Cambridge, MA: Harvard University Press; London: Heinemann, 1946).

the reign of Solomon, when Israel flourished politically and socially'.[5]
Von Rad, a theologian and Bible scholar, writing some 50 years ago,
similarly described the reign of Solomon as 'an age of intensive en-
lightenment', or 'a Solomonic humanism',[6] a period of openness to the
world and a lively literary output in various forms. Those who support
the view that biblical historiography began in the tenth century BCE,
namely, during the united kingdom, note that there is no mention of a
scribe in the administration of King Saul, whereas in the court of David
there are references to a scribe named Seraiah or Sheva (2 Sam. 8.17
and 20.25).[7] In Solomon's court there were already two: 'Elihoreph and
Ahijah sons of Shisha—scribes' (1 Kgs 4.3). Evidently the role of
scribes in the senior administration of the united monarchy arose from
the need to maintain its proper function. The beginning of biblical historiography was naturally attributed by different scholars to these early
royal scribes.

But did the scribes of the royal court write the biblical history that we
know? It seems to me that there is no way to test this hypothesis, and I
am inclined to disagree with the widely held view that biblical historiography began during the united kingdom. Biblical historiography is
distinguished by being unlike the chronicles, and not praising the acts
of the kings. It is unique in that it emphasizes the role of God and
exposes the weaknesses and sins of the various leaders. It is doubtful
that any court scribe would have written such compositions, and doubtful that any king would have kept an administration that defamed him
and described him as an adulterer and murderer (e.g. in the case of
David with Bathsheba and Uriah: 2 Sam. 11–12); as exploiting his
people in his building enterprises and being swayed by his wives (in the
case of Solomon: 1 Kgs 4–11), as failing because he listened to the
advice of 'children' (Rehoboam: 1 Kgs 12) or, because he 'put so many

---

5.   In *Eretz-Israel* 1 (1951), pp. 85-88 (Heb.); repr. in U.M.D. Cassuto, 'The
Beginning of Historiography among the Israelites', in *idem, Biblical and Canaanite
Literatures: Studies on the Bible and Ancient Orient*, I (Jerusalem: Magnes Press,
1972 [Heb.]), pp. 12-19. The quotation is taken from p. 19.
6.   G. von Rad, *Old Testament Theology*. I. *The Theology of Israel's Historical
Traditions* (trans. D.M.G. Stalker; Edinburgh: Oliver & Boyd, 1962), p. 55; see
also *idem*, 'The Beginnings of Historical Writing in Ancient Israel', in *idem, The
Problem of the Hexateuch and Other Essays* (trans. E.W. Trueman Dicken;
Edinburgh: Oliver & Boyd, 1966), pp. 166-204.
7 .   In 1 Chron. 18.16 he is named Shavsha.

innocent persons to death that he filled Jerusalem with blood from end to end—besides the sin he committed in causing Judah to do what was displeasing to the Lord' (the case of Manasseh: 2 Kgs 21.16)—and this is not the end of the list. In other words, it is difficult to imagine an ancient king of such extraordinary tolerance that he would keep objective-to-hostile scribes who did not spare him their harsh criticism, and who instead of glorifying his achievements chose to emphasize his sins and failures.

Indeed, the novelist Stefan Heym, who lived in East Germany before the reunification, was struck by the paradox of anti-monarchical courtly writing. His novel *The King David Report* suggests that the story of David as it appears in the book of Samuel is in fact a much softened version of events, the compromise version produced by the courtly scribe who was compelled to erase many of David's sins and defeats.[8] The novel suggests that had the writer written the truth and not made great efforts to cleanse the king's reputation, the picture would have been considerably worse. Though Heym uses the reign of David as depicted in the book of Samuel to criticize the East German regime and its official histories, there is no doubt that his imagination was stirred by the strange phenomenon of a biblical courtly history that did not flatter the ruler.

In my view, it is unreasonable to attribute the start of Israelite historiography to the royal scribes of the united kingdom in the tenth century BCE, which would mean that this was courtly writing produced by scribes who were the king's dependents. It is more reasonable to assume that it was written outside the court. We must therefore enquire when this became possible, or rather, when literary writing became possible outside the king's court.

The conclusion that biblical historiography was not courtly gives rise to further questions. First, when did Israelites who were not specially trained royal scribes become literate? It must be kept in mind that in ancient times literacy was never widespread but always confined to a few professionals. If literature was being written beyond the confines of the royal court, does this mean that there was a circle of literate people other than the ruling aristocracy?

8. S. Heym, *The King David Report* (trans. S. Heym; New York: Putnam, 1973 [German edition 1972]).

Second, when did circumstances combine to give rise to a new literary genre, namely historiography, which was previously unknown in Israel and the entire region?

Third, who were the creators of this new genre which, as we shall see, boasted a sophisticated writing style with marked aesthetic qualities?

The answer to the first question must be sought in archaeology, the available findings of which indicate that reading and writing began to spread in Judah and Israel only in the eighth century BCE. Aaron Demsky, in his study on literacy,[9] stressed that an unmistakable mark of a varied literate population is the unprofessional appearance of documents, or the existence of documents which were plainly meant to be read by the public at large. Demsky also noted four criteria that show that the kingdom of Judah had a literate society during the last 150 years before its downfall, that is, from the eighth century BCE. He deduced this from the following:

1. The epigraphic findings, chiefly personal seals, small inscribed weights and *lmek* seal impressions.
2. The fact that this period saw the appearance of a 'vulgar script', suggesting writers of common rather than courtly background.
3. The analysis of the written findings, showing that many of them were written by laymen—artisans such as vintners and wine-growers, merchants, potters and the like—for their own purposes, possibly by their own hand.
4. The written record of the classical prophetic literature (= the writing prophets), which was contemporary and meant to be read by the public at large.[10]

Nadav Na'aman takes a similar position when he points out that

> it is no longer possible, after so many years of intensive archaeological exploration throughout the kingdoms of Israel and Judah, to speak of coincidental finding. Jerusalem, for example, has been intensively explored for the past 150 years, with excavations in all parts of the city. Nevertheless, not a single inscription has been found from before the end of the eighth century BCE. It cannot be a coincidence that starting from

---

9. A. Demsky, 'Literacy in Israel and among Neighboring Peoples in the Biblical Period' (Thesis submitted to the Hebrew University, Jerusalem, 1976 [Heb.]).
10. Demsky, 'Literacy', pp. 118-39.

the seventh century written findings begin to proliferate throughout Judah. The archaeological evidence testifies to the spread of writing.[11]

To sum up, it is possible to assume that from the eighth century BCE onwards there was a literate public which was not necessarily part of the ruling establishment. This means that the writing of biblical history, not being courtly writing, could not have been written before the eighth century BCE, which means that it was not written in the courts of David and Solomon as part of their administrative activities. I argue that the independent, indeed critical, character of this literature, which could not be of service to the rulers, suggests a circle of writers outside the royal court. This led to the question as to when did literacy spread beyond the confines of the king's court and out of the control of the professional scribes who were trained to serve the royal administration. The archaeological findings show that such circumstances could have arisen only from the eighth century BCE onwards.

Let us now examine this date from another viewpoint, by asking when the circumstances arose that gave birth to this new literary genre, namely, historiography (our second question).

In ancient Greece, for example, the main impulse for historical writing was an event that became a turning-point, and a sense that the world would never again be what it was. It impelled people to examine the past and to document it comprehensively, so that future societies would be able to learn its lessons. There is no doubt that the writing of Herodotus and Thucydides was affected by the historical events that shook the very foundations of the Greek society in which they lived. Herodotus opened his book, which he wrote after he encountered and fought against the Persians, with the statement:

> What Herodotus the Halicarnassian has learnt by inquiry is here set forth: in order that so the memory of the past may not be blotted out from among men by time, and that great and marvellous deeds done by

11. N. Na'aman, 'Historiography, the Fashioning of the Collective Memory, and the Establishment of Historical Consciousness in Israel in the Late Monarchical Period' (Heb.), *Zion* 60.4 (1995), pp. 449-72. The only previous evidence of alphabetic script in Israel is Gezer Calendar from the tenth century BCE; however, it reflects the Canaanite or the Phoenician tradition. For more bibliography on this subject, see I. Young, 'The Style of Gezer Calendar and some "Archaic Biblical Hebrew" Passages', *VT* 42 (1992), pp. 362-75.

Greeks and foreigners and especially the reason why they warred against
each other may not lack renown.[12]

Thucydides, who wrote not long after, and had witnessed the conflict
between Athens and Sparta and feared the rise of the latter and its
allies, was convinced that writing the history of the war was a lesson
that ought to be taught. He opens his work on the Peloponnesian war by
stating: 'And, indeed, it has been composed, not as a prize-essay to be
heard for the moment, but as a possession for all times'.[13]

Another example, closer to our subject, is the historiographical en-
terprise of Josephus Flavius's *Antiquities of the Jews*, which he wrote
following the destruction of the Second Temple by the Romans.[14]

In the light of these examples and others, I believe that the most decisive historical event to threaten Judah since the inception of the
monarchy and its division into two kingdoms was the defeat of the
northern kingdom of Israel by Assyria and the deportation of some of
its inhabitants (720 BCE). The Assyrian conquest, with its methods of
annexation and the transfer of populations, affected the contemporary
world-view, shook the foundations of existence and gave rise to a sense
that the world of the past, with its familiar values and features, had collapsed.[15] The conquered kingdoms were superseded by a huge empire,
which imposed its power and its culture on the territories it annexed.
Thus, in addition to the immediate political and economic effects, the
conquered nations also experienced the destruction of their national
cultures. The fate of the northern kingdom of Israel, and life under
Assyrian rule, produced in Judah an existential dread, resulting in
national heart-searching and a cultural revolution. This state of affairs
was revealed in a number of developments which took place from the
middle of the eighth century onwards:

1.   The rise of the preaching prophets, also called the 'classical
      prophets' or the 'writing prophets', in the middle of the eighth
      century, and the writing down of their sermons probably soon

---

12.   Herodotus 1.1 (A.D. Godley [trans.], *Herodotus: In Four Volumes*, I [LCL;
Cambridge, MA: Harvard University Press; London: Heinemann, 1946], p. 3).

13.   Thucydides, 1.22.

14.   On the reasons for his writing, see his introduction in Josephus, *Ant.* 1.1.

15.   For information on the system and its application, see B. Oded, *Mass Deportation and Deportees in the Neo-Assyrian Empire* (Wiesbaden: L. Reichert, 1979).

after. Amos and Hosea belong to the first phase, Isaiah and Micah to the second.[16]

2. Religious reforms, the first of which is ascribed to the reign of Hezekiah (2 Kgs 18.4), that is, to the final quarter of the eighth century,[17] and its continuation in the centralizing reform under Josiah, about 100 years later (622 BCE).[18]

3. The *collection* and copying of wise sayings, which is a prominent part of the wisdom literature, as attested by Prov. 25.1— 'These too are the proverbs of Solomon, which the men of king Hezekiah king of Judah copied'—suggesting that the proverbs were copied in the final quarter of the eighth century BCE.[19]

It is, therefore, a reasonable assumption that at this time there was also much law-making activity, that new laws were promulgated and existing ones reformulated and collated in a book. It was probably this activity which produced the book of Deuteronomy, which most scholars believe to have been the book discovered in 'the repair of the house' that preceded and motivated Josiah's reform (2 Kgs 22.1-10).[20]

16. I.L. Seeligmann ('On the History and Nature of Prophecy in Israel' [Heb.], *Eretz-Israel* 3 [1954], pp. 125-32 [131]) emphasizes the historical background of classical prophecy and he praises J. Wellhausen for describing in his early writings (article in *Jahrbücher für deutsche Theologie* 21 [1876]) the connection between classical prophecy and the rise of Assyria. I have not been able either to find the title or to read Wellhausen's article.

17. On the attempt to deny this reform, see N. Na'aman, 'The Debated Historicity of Hezekiah's Reform in the Light of Historical and Archaeological Research', *ZAW* 107 (1995), pp. 179-95. However, I am convinced that the mention of a 'bronze serpent that Moses had made', as an object that the Israelites worshipped even in the days of David and Solomon, does not reflect a Deuteronomistic tendency, and may have represented reality.

18. This reform, too, is denied by some scholars; see, e.g., H.D. Hoffmann, *Reform und Reformen: Untersuchungen zu einem Grundthema der deuteronomistischen Geschichtsschreibung* (ATANT, 66; Zürich: Theologischer Verlag, 1980).

19. C.H. Toy (*The Book of Proverbs* [ICC; Edinburgh: T. & T. Clark, 1959 (1899)], p. 458) suggests that 'the fall of Samaria would have led the men of Judah to collect the literature of the northern kingdom, and our Section has in fact, been regarded as Ephraimitic'. However, Toy himself does not accept this.

20. W.M.L. de Wette, in his dissertation ('Dissertatio critico-exegetica qua Deuteronomium a prioribus Pentateuchi Libris diversum, alius cuiusdam recentioris auctioris opus esse monstratur; quam...auctoritate amplissimi philosophorum ordinis

In consequence of these events and the literary activity, it is quite likely that some circles felt the need to examine thoroughly the nation's past and interpret the present in its light. The impact of Assyrian imperialism upon their world forced the thinkers of the age—of whom a dominant group were the classical prophets—to consider the relative standing of the God of Israel, the master of the nation's destiny, vis-à-vis the gods of other nations (such as Assyria), that seemed to be taking over the world and determining Israel's fate as well. Their solution was to depict a historical scene wherein a single deity ruled the world and was responsible for punishing Israel by means of other nations, as well as for liberating it from their power. This solution, presupposing the existence of a universal deity, is characteristic of the classical prophets, and may be found in Amos and Isaiah, two prophets from Judah who flourished just before the downfall of the northern kingdom of Israel. Amos's prophecy of nations, which opens with the words, 'For three transgressions of Damascus, for four, I will not revoke it' (Amos 1.3-5), supposes that the God of Israel chastises the other nations according to the same principles of justice. God's universal dominion is likewise implied in his prophecy about the settlement of the different peoples: 'True, I brought Israel up from the land of Egypt, but also the Philistines from Caphtor, and the Aramaeans from Kir' (Amos 9.7). Isaiah describes Assyrian imperialism as temporary and as part of God's design: 'But when my Lord has carried out all his purpose on Mount Zion and in Jerusalem, He will punish the majestic pride and overbearing arrogance of the king of Assyria. For he thought, by the might of my hand have I wrought it, by my skill, for I am clever: I have erased the borders of the peoples... (Isa. 10.12-13). This connection between the historical circumstances of Assyrian imperial expansion and the emphasis on the universality of God, as the one who masters and pilots human history and watches over it, characterizes the prophets' interpretation of contemporary events—an observation first made by the nineteenth-century German scholar Julius Wellhausen.[21]

---

pro venia legendi AD XXVIII' [Jena, 1805]), was the first to discover the correlation between the law of cult centralization and Josiah's reform, and to conclude that Deuteronomy was written earlier, i.e. in the seventh century.

21. See n. 16 above, and also J. Guttmann, *Philosophies of Judaism: The History of Jewish Philosophy from Biblical Times to Franz Rosenzweig* (trans. D.W. Silverman; New York: Holt, Rinehart & Winston, 1964 [original German 1933]), pp. 5-6.

In the light of the above, it seems to me that this new vision of the world and of God as its pilot needed a new genre to express itself—namely, historiography, which here means the writing of a history that examines the destiny of Israel in relation to its God and to its neighbours. Moreover, since these circumstances came about in a period of growing literacy, it could break out of the confines of the royal court and serve intellectual circles, prophets such as Amos, Isaiah and Jeremiah, writers like Baruch the son of Neriah (Jer. 32.12 and elsewhere), or the family of Shaphan the scribe, a member of the Jerusalem aristocracy, who was associated with the discovery of the reform book in the reign of Josiah (2 Kgs 22.3-10; see also Jer. 36.10-11, 29.3; Ezek. 8.11; 2 Chron. 34.15-20; and elsewhere).

This, then, is the answer to the third question in the previous chapter, concerning the social background of the authors. It must have been a circle of people who sought to influence the king and who opposed his policies. These would include, for example, Ahikam, the son of Shaphan, one of Jeremiah's supporters (Jer. 26.24), and likewise his son Gedaliah, who was appointed by the Babylonians to rule over the populace that had not been sent into exile (Jer. 39.14). It would seem that these people—among them scribes, prophets and priests—who were critical of the ruler, dared to support a policy which did not accord with the official one, and at the same time dared to write history and explore the past in justification of their political and social thinking.

I mentioned two theories regarding the beginning of historiography in Israel: one dates it back to the tenth century BCE, associating it with Solomon's court, while the other dates it to the end of the eighth century BCE, and associates it with social circles outside the royal court.

It should also be noted that following Noth's book on the subject, published in 1943, most critical scholars today believe that historical writing in Israel began soon after the fall of the First Temple (586 BCE).[22] They argue that the downfall of the kingdom of Judah was the

---

22. M. Noth, *Überlieferungsgeschichtliche Studien* (Tübingen: M. Niemeyer, 1943); ET *The Deuteronomistic History* (JSOTSup, 15; Sheffield: JSOT Press, 1981). Lately, J. Van Seters, *In Search of History: Historiography in the Ancient World and the Origins of Biblical History* (New Haven: Yale University Press, 1983). Others suggest that there are two stages in this composition: the earlier one is close to Josiah's reign and the later one is postexilic; e.g. F.M. Cross, *Canaanite Myth and Hebrew Epic* (Cambridge, MA: Harvard University Press, 1973), pp. 274-89; R.D. Nelson, *The Double Redaction of the Deuteronomistic History* (JSOTSup, 18;

event that triggered historical writing, and its fruit was the Deuteronomistic composition encompassing Deuteronomy, Joshua, Judges, Samuel and Kings. It rested largely on previous and primal sources, which
it utilized in the new work that scholars have named the Deuteronomistic Composition because of its close association with the book of
Deuteronomy and its ideology: 'When he is seated on his royal throne,
he shall have a copy of this Teaching written for him on a scroll by the
levitical priests' (Deut. 17.18). The name Deuteronomy derives from
the Greek translation of the words 'a copy of this Teaching'. This
composition was intended to present the history of the people of Israel,
from the exodus to the destruction of the temple, and to explain the
downfall of the kingdoms of Judah and Israel as resulting from the
people's violation of the covenant with God, and their failure to obey
the law of Deuteronomy.

According to this theory, all the books in the composition (Deuteronomy through 2 Kings) share the same ideology. It therefore tends to
emphasize their common qualities, downplay their differences and
stress the similarities between them. For example, an important precept
in Deuteronomy is the centralization of worship (Deut. 12), which by
implication forbids the holding of religious rituals in local 'high places'.
There is no doubt that this precept is observed throughout the historical
narrative in the book of Kings, which is why the description of King
Solomon sacrificing in Gibeon is preceded by an apologetic note that it
happened before the temple was built: 'The people, however, continued
to offer sacrifices at the open shrines, because up to that time no house
had been built for the name of the Lord. And Solomon, though he loved
the Lord and followed the practices of his father David, also sacrificed
and offered at the shrines' (1 Kgs 3.2-4). However, in the books of
Judges and Samuel, where various places of worship are mentioned, no
such reservations or statements are voiced, nor is there any hint of a
future need to centralize worship and eliminate the high places and
local altars.

We may, therefore, reasonably question the widespread assumption
that the books of Judges and Samuel also reflect and represent the
Deuteronomistic world-view.

Sheffield: JSOT Press, 1981); and others. Some scholars tend to date this composition to a much later period, long after the fall of the First Temple, as for example,
P.R. Davies, *In Search of 'Ancient Israel'* (JSOTSup, 148; Sheffield: JSOT Press,
1992).

One more example: according to Deuteronomy, the centre of worship is only the habitation of God's name (Deut. 12.5, 11 and elsewhere), whereas David wishes to build a house for God to dwell in (2 Sam. 7.5). David, like the people of Israel in the battle of Eben-ezer (1 Sam. 4.3; see also chs. 5–6), expresses a concrete conception of the deity that Deuteronomy militates against. These points, being part of a whole argument (which will be dealt with extensively in the following chapters), show that the books of Judges and Samuel were not quite historical compositions reflecting the full ideological system of Deuteronomy, though they do contain ideas which Deuteronomy subsequently developed. In other words, if Judges and Samuel basically do not express Deuternomistic ideas, it must mean that their author was not familiar with these ideas. And if we accept that Deuteronomy was composed in the seventh century BCE, a little before Josiah's reform of 622, this would mean that Israelite historiography existed even before the writing of Deuteronomy, and may be connected with events at the end of the eighth century BCE.

Therefore, I would conclude that the beginning of historiography in Israel took place not in the time of Solomon, nor was it connected to the fall of the kingdom of Judah, but was a reaction of Judaean society to the destruction wreaked upon the region by Assyria at the end of the eighth century BCE. In any event, it predates Herodotus's historiography by at least two centuries or more.

In the following chapters I will discuss whether biblical historiography was devoted to a particular ideology, or represented various ideologies associated with the periods of writing.

Chapter 3

THE BOOK OF JUDGES, AND HISTORY AS IDEOLOGY

In this chapter the discussion is devoted to the book of Judges and the manner in which it defines God's place in history. I have chosen Judges because it seems to me to be an early attempt at a systematic description of the chain of events, rather than a single occurrence in a historical period, and an examination of the role of the deity throughout the period and its problems.[1]

I have said that the historiographic biblical compositions are not homogeneous. They were produced at different times, some as far back as the eighth century BCE, and some from the Persian period.[2] Yet all of them used past events to serve their ideas. When biblical writers sought to describe the past, they built the picture around a particular idea, or a systematic, coherent set of ideas. These writers were not impelled by a desire to get at the truth, or to document past events, but by the need to propound an idea or an ideological system, and to use the past as a proving-ground for their ideas. That is why we find different historical accounts of the same period in the Bible—it is the result of using the same proving-ground to serve different ideas. I shall come back to this point in the discussion of the book of Chronicles.

In Chapter 1 I argued that biblical historical narrative replaced mythology, and that in monotheistic thought the acts of the gods gave way to the acts of human beings under God's dominance. Instead of

1. This chapter is largely based on my Hebrew book *The Book of Judges: The Art of Editing* (Jerusalem and Tel Aviv: The Bialik Institute, 1992), published in English under this title by E.J. Brill, Leiden, 1999. References are to the English edition.

2. In analysing the book of Judges as pre-Deuteronomistic (meaning that it was written before Deuteronomy) at the end of the eighth century BCE, I come close to the view held by C.F. Burney, *The Book of Judges* (New York: Ktav, 1970 [1903, 1918]).

tales about the nature of different gods, their loves and jealousies, their wars and habits, the ways of placating them and what might be expected of them, there emerged tales about the relations of God and his people and divine interventions in human history. Each of the historical books in the Bible seeks to examine this system and to understand the principles of the ways of God. They ask questions such as: How is God's just rule expressed? Is he guided by the principle of reward and punishment? When does he intervene directly and when by means of agents? Does God punish and reward his creatures at once, or does he act in the long term—in other words, is the sinful community punished for its own sins, or do future generations pay for its sins? Or, in biblical terms, is it a case of God 'visiting the guilt of the parents upon the children, upon the third and upon the fourth generations' (Exod. 20.5; cf. 34.7; Num. 14.18; Deut. 5.9), or is it rather 'a person shall be put to death only for his own crime' (Deut. 24.16; cf. 2 Kgs 14.6; 2 Chron. 25.4)? Does a ruler bear public responsibility? How does the ruler and the ruled know God's will?—and many more questions of this kind.

Naturally, the presence of such questions at the heart of a historical description created narratives that cannot be detached from their ideological bias. Let us see how this applies to the book of Judges.

The book seeks to show that the course of history is shaped by the interaction between God and his people, conducted by means of omens. The omens are a system of signs, direct or indirect, sent by God, showing his intervention and the manner in which he directs the course of events. According to the book of Judges, these omens were given in the time of the judges in two forms: one, by a cyclic principle, which is common to much of the book, and the other by depicting the wars of the judges as God's wars and the judges as God's emissaries.[3]

First let us see how the cyclic principle works in the structure of the book. The principle is already presented in the book's opening as part

---

3. Most of the critical scholars suppose that the development of the cyclic principle is the work of the Deuteronomistic historians, and that the tales of the judges are earlier and based on old traditions. See the detailed concluding research of W. Richter, *Traditionsgeschichtliche Untersuchungen zum Richterbuch* (BibB, 18; Bonn: P. Hanstein, 1963); *idem, Die Bearbeitungen des 'Retterbuches' in der deuteronomischen Epoche* (BibB, 21; Bonn: P. Hanstein, 1964). But see n. 2 above.

of its 'exposition', that is, as one of the elements that needs to be presented to the readers from the start (Judg. 2.11-19).[4] It states that history in the time of the judges moved in periodic cycles of sin, punishment and deliverance (= liberation), followed by a period of calm under
the leadership of the judge. The opening description is very generalized,
noting neither the length of the periods of subjugation nor the names of
the liberators. Throughout this time, from the judgeship of Othniel, son
of Kenaz (Judg. 3.7-11), to that of Samson (Judg. 13–16), there are also
cycles that consist of five phases: sin, punishment, a cry to God,
liberation and peace. This scheme comprises the following phases: the
children of Israel sin against God by worshipping other gods; God
punishes them with subjugation to another nation; unable to bear the
conqueror's yoke, they cry out to God; God sends a deliverer who frees
them from their oppressors; there follows a period of political peace,
until the people sin again and the cycle repeats itself. The first three or
four phases precede the detailed description of the act of deliverance,
and the final phase of calm ends it. [5] Thus, these cyclical stages form a
framework for each story of liberation, giving prominence to the role of
God in the salvation. When God is sinned against he punishes; when he
is appealed to, he raises up a deliverer, endowing him with his spirit.
Finally, when the people sin again, God replaces the stage of peace
with punishment. Thus God himself, in response to his people's
conduct, is responsible for the existence of the cyclical system, namely,
to the course of history.

It should be noted that not all five phases are mentioned every time.
The general preamble to the book refers only to four (Judg. 2.11-19).
Here the phase of crying to God is left out, and its absence in the
preamble emphasizes the misconduct of the people—they did not even
turn to God for help—and God's tolerance and charity: though the children of Israel kept turning away from him and disobeying him, he continued to save them by means of the judges.[6]

---

4.   The exposition of Judges contains some distinctive materials which encom-
pass chs. 1–3.6. For a detailed analysis, see my *The Book of Judges*, pp. 120-66.
According to R.H. O'Connell (*The Rhetoric of the Book of Judges*, Leiden: E.J.
Brill, 1996), this is the 'Judges' double prologue', while the unit 2.11-19 is part of
the second prologue, intended to serve as a religio-historical paradigm.
5.   In *The Book of Judges* I show that the time of the judges, as described in the
book of Judges, is composed of seven cycles (pp. 44-45).
6.   All five stages are mentioned only in the stories of Othniel (Judg. 3.7-11)

Let us examine the description of the judgeship of Othniel, son of Kenaz (Judg. 3.7-11), as an example of the five phases. It opens with the phase of sin: 'The Israelites did what was offensive to the Lord; they ignored the Lord their God and worshipped the Baalim and the Asheroth' (v. 7). Then comes the punishment phase: 'The Lord became incensed at Israel and surrendered them to king Chushan-rishathaim of Aram-naharaim; and the Israelites were subject to Chushan-rishathaim for eight years' (v. 8). This is followed by the third phase, that of crying out to God: 'The Israelites cried out to the Lord' (v. 9a); then the phase of deliverence: 'and the Lord raised a champion for the Israelites to deliver them: Othniel the Kenizzite, a younger kinsman of Caleb. The spirit of the Lord descended upon him and he became Israel's chieftain. He went out to war, and the Lord delivered king Chushan-rishathaim of Aram into his hands. He prevailed over Chushan-rishathaim' (vv. 9b-10). The fifth and final phase, that of peace, concludes the tale: 'And the land had peace for forty years. And Othniel the son of Kenaz died' (v. 11).[7]

So much for the cyclic framework that stresses God's supervision over history, and the manner in which the sins of the people cause its wheels to turn. Yet even in this brief passage of Othniel, son of Kenaz, we notice that the phase of deliverance is proportionately more detailed (almost two verses). In other stories this phase becomes a whole story in itself. In the tale of Ehud, son of Gera, for example, (Judg. 3.12-30), the phase of the deliverance expatiates on Ehud's manoeuvres; how, armed with a double-edged dagger, he managed to penetrate not only the residence of Eglon, king of Moab, but also the cool upper chamber where the king was sitting alone. There Ehud was alone with the king, forced him to rise from his seat and stabbed him. He then made good his escape while the king's men tarried, summoned his army, reached the fords of Jordan and captured the entire Moabite army.[8] Here less than five verses (12-15 and 30b) are devoted to the four phases of the

---

and Ehud (Judg. 3.12-30). But whenever the framework misses a stage, it is possible to deduce the reasons— as, e.g., in the case of Deborah and Barak (chs. 4–5), where the stage of raising up the deliverer is missing because the story is presented as a riddle. Therefore, who is the actual deliverer? This case and all the others are analysed in my book, *The Book of Judges*.

7. Verse 11b fits the KJV.

8. This story of deliverance is dealt with further in this chapter and in greater detail at the end of the book, pp. 109-113.

framework, whereas the phase of deliverance is described in fourteen to fifteen verses. In other tales of deliverance, such as those of Gideon or Jephthah, the ratio is even more extreme, with several chapters devoted to the phase of deliverance.

I have noted that the shaping of the accounts of the judges' wars and of the personalities of the deliverers also serve the historian's purpose, by way of the signs or omens revealing God's action in history. The liberator is always a person who has been sent by God. Even if to start with he is unaware that God has sent him, as in the case of Ehud, he becomes aware in process of the liberation that he is acting upon the will and with the power of God: '"Follow me closely", he said, "for the Lord has delivered your enemies, the Moabites, into your hands"' (Judg. 3.28). Two examples show that the liberator is depicted as an instrument of providence. First, Gideon, who liberated his people, is shown as needing signs and proofs that God is with him, has sent him and will help him. Without the series of omens and signs—such as his encounter with the 'angel of the Lord' (Judg. 6.11-21), his dialogues with God (6.22-26; 7.1-8), the affair of the fleece of wool (6.36-40) and the dream of the Midianite soldier (7.9-15a)—it is doubtful if the sceptical and wavering Gideon would have gone to war (7.15b–8.21). Secondly, Samson, by contrast, is depicted as being one moved by the spirit of God, and exploits every pretext and opportunity (14.4) to act against the Philistines (14.19–16.30).

The manner in which the wars of the judges are told also stresses the role of God. One example is the war of Deborah, Barak and Jael against Jabin, king of Canaan, and his army commander Sisera. Here the role of Barak, who is supposed to be the hero of the war, is overshadowed by two women: Deborah who sends him into battle, and Jael who kills the Canaanite captain for him. This is foreseen by the prophecy of Deborah at the start of the story: 'There will be no glory for you in the course you are taking, for then the Lord will deliver Sisera into the hands of a woman' (Judg. 4.9). Later this point is stressed again: 'And the Lord threw Sisera and all his chariots and army into a panic before the onslaught of Barak. Sisera leaped from his chariot and fled on foot' (4.15). The sceptical reader may well wonder what, then, was Barak's part in this battle. He goes to war with a prophetess at his elbow who sends him into the battlefield; when he gets there he finds that God has already stunned the Canaanite army, and all he has to do is to chase Sisera and kill him; and when he finds him he discovers that Jael has already carried out the task. In the war of Gideon against the Midianites the narrator stresses that it is God's will that the war be conducted by the few against the many, for only thus will the people recognize that God had aided them: 'The Lord said to Gideon, "You have too many troops with you for me to deliver Midian into their hands; Israel might claim for themselves the glory due to me, thinking, 'our own hand has brought us victory'"' (Judg. 7.2).

The book of Judges shows God as intervening directly at every stage in history. He sends angels and omens and his spirit descends upon the heroes. But even without these obvious signs, the conclusion that God has directed events is unavoidable, as in the tale of Ehud's devices.[9] The success of his tactics, despite the hazards and dangers, convinces Ehud that God himself has delivered the Moabite army into his hands, as he says to his troops, 'Follow me closely, for the Lord has delivered your enemies, the Moabites, into your hands' (Judg. 3.28). Moreover, the statement that God has sent Ehud (Judg. 3.15) draws the reader's attention to the fine balance between human devices and divine support. As the psalmist puts it, 'Unless the Lord builds the house, its builders labour in vain on it; unless the Lord watches over the city, the watchman keeps vigil in vain' (Ps. 127.1).

Thus the chain of events—namely, the course of history—is controlled by God, who directs it according to the conduct of the people. In this way Israel is responsible for its own fate and may determine the course of history. It depends entirely on the people's perseverance and faithfulness to God. History serves as the proving-ground between God and his people, so that its course reveals God's demands, the people's conduct and the nature of the deliverance whose agents are not mere heroes, but messenger-heroes.

The cyclic phenomenon raises the questions of how the time of the judges will ever end, and how the wheel of cycles can ever stop turning. The ending of the book indicates that the answer lies in changing the system—from sporadic liberators to the permanence of monarchy, with its dynastic continuity. The need for a continuous leadership was already given expression in the days of Gideon, when the men of Israel came to him with the request, 'Rule over us—you, your son, and your

9. See my article, 'The Story of Ehud (Judges 3.12-30): The Form and the Message', in J.C. Exum (ed.), *Signs and Wonders: Biblical Texts in Literary Focus* (Semeia Studies; Atlanta: Scholars Press, 1989), pp. 97-123.

grandson as well; for you have saved us from the Midianites' (Judg. 8.22). Gideon refuses, saying, 'I will not rule over you myself, nor shall my son rule over you; the Lord alone shall rule over you' (Judg. 8.23). However, it transpired that divine rule[10] did not stop the cycles, and the book ends with the conclusion that monarchy is imperative, because otherwise there is anarchy and social chaos: 'In those days there was no king in Israel; everyone did as he pleased' (Judg. 17.6, 21.25; see also 18.1a, 19.1a). The absence of continuous human government led to an increasing deterioration in many aspects of life, as shown in the story of Micah's graven image (Judg. 17–18), which criticizes the social, political and cultural state of affairs. The ingratitude of the landless tribe of the Danites to Micah demonstrates the state of anarchy in which the strong prevail over the weak. The author of the book of Judges clearly believes that this situation may only be cured by appointing a king, rather than by means of judges. It is noteworthy that the last judges in the book are somewhat disappointing, for example, Jephthah, who sacrificed his daughter and was responsible for a civil war, and Samson, who died in captivity and did not save his people from the Philistines. The realization that it is necessary to have a king was therefore an important lesson drawn from the time of God's rule and the leadership of the judges. God and his people realize that there must be a continuous national leadership which would bear the responsibility for its position and all that it entails.

To sum up: the book of Judges has told us how the cycle of phases and the acts of deliverance by the judges sustained the relations between God and his people throughout that period. Whenever the people turned to their God they were answered and delivered, and whenever they turned away from God they were punished. The recurring historical and cyclical sequence indirectly reveals the divine operation and its motives. Likewise, most of the acts of salvation, depicting the judge as the emissary of God who acts in his name and on his behalf, represent omens which point out the presence and the intervention of the guiding providence. In other words, the wish to underline the divine omens—namely, the nature of history as a process governed by discernible laws rather than as a random series of events—is the reason that most of the events described in this book are organized in cycles.

10. On the meaning of divine rule, defined by some who follow Buber as 'kingdom of God' (M. Buber, *Kingship of God* [trans. R. Scheimann; London: Allen & Unwin, 3rd edn, 1967]), see my *The Book of Judges*, pp. 96-99.

This wish also accounts for the fact that throughout the cycles the bulk of the narratives is devoted to the acts of deliverance. The reader is given tendentious information, selected and elaborated so as to depict the period as rich in omens, illustrating God's providence and his rule, and the conduct expected from his people.

An examination of the time of the judges leads the reader to another conclusion connected with the nature of leadership, from judges to monarchy: while the system of judges emphasized the role of God, the system of monarchy assigned the central and crucial position to the king, which was inevitably interpreted as rejecting the kingdom of God (1 Sam. 8.7). And indeed the book of Samuel is devoted to the examination of the role of monarchy in the life of Israel, and the position of the king beside God. If the reader of the book of Judges is led to conclude that monarchy is an ideal solution, the book of Samuel, which describes the rise and establishment of kingship, teaches another lesson in the understanding of monarchy in Israel—as we shall see in the next chapter.

Chapter 4

THE TEST OF MONARCHY IN HISTORY'S PROVING-GROUND

The previous chapter dealt with the book of Judges as one of the earliest historical texts in the Bible, devoted to the examination of God's role as the pilot of history. As a result, the period of the judges is depicted as a sequence of cycles expressing the connection between God and his people. The people sinned and God punished them, the people cried out and God sent them liberators. These liberators had only a certain amount of influence upon events, and the book concludes with the expectation of the monarchy to come.

The institution of monarchy is the main subject of the book of Samuel. In it the reigns of Saul and David are looked at as samples for testing the merits and defects of this form of government. Continuing the metaphor of the historical account as a proving-ground, we might say that in the book of Samuel the proving-ground is used to test the place of monarchy in a monotheistic culture, where the omnipotent status of the deity may be threatened by the omnipotent power of the king. The present chapter will therefore look at the manner in which the book of Samuel contends with the idea of monarchy and with the essential outlook it generates.

The concept of monarchy needs to be examined closely and its limitations studied, because in the ancient Near East, the birthplace of Israel and its culture, the king was regarded in association with the gods, and even as part of the system of creation. In Egypt the king was himself a god, or the son of the sun god; in Mesopotamia he appeared as god's agent, acting in his name and on his behalf, and sometimes as god's priest. Mesopotamian texts reveal a world-view in which the human kingdom existed to serve the needs of the gods and maintain their worship. The king stood next to the gods in the hierarchy, or as a mediator between the gods and men, and his rule was perceived both as part of human existence and the embodiment of god's will and grace.[1]

By contrast, biblical historiography expresses a cautious and uncertain approach to monarchy.[2] In the first place, monarchy does not appear to be an inseparable part of the life of the nation, but as a relatively late development in its history. The early leaders, such as Moses and Joshua, were not kings. The judges were chosen by God for specific missions, and were criticized whenever they behaved like kings and transferred their rule to their sons. This is what happened in the case of Abimelech, the son of Gideon (Judg. 9), whose kingship is described as a tyranny; and so it is in the case of Joel and Abiah, the sons of Samuel, who are characterized as corrupt perverters of justice (1 Sam. 8.1-3). In fact, already in the book of Judges it is possible to discern two distinct approaches to monarchy.[3] One takes a critical view of monarchy and its representatives, as expressed briefly in Gideon's statement and broadly and by concrete means in the parable of Jotham. Gideon turned down the people's request that he become king, saying, 'I will not rule over you myself, nor shall my son rule over you; the Lord alone shall rule over you' (Judg. 8.23); his son Jotham described the kingship of Abimelech as useless and even harmful. The olive tree, the fig tree and the vine refused to reign, but the thorny bramble, which is quick to catch fire and burn its surroundings, was quite willing (Judg. 9.1-15). Nevertheless, as we have seen, the ending of the book of Judges points to monarchy as the answer to all the troubles of the age. It reflects not only approval, but also a recognition of the need for monarchy and the absence of any other ruling solution.

An ambivalent or equivocal approach to monarchy, appreciating the need for it while illustrating its negative aspects and the importance of restricting its power, lies at the very heart of the book of Samuel. On

1.   See C.J. Gadd, *Ideas of Divine Rule in the Ancient East* (London: Oxford University Press, 1943); H. Frankfort, *Kingship and the Gods* (Chicago: University of Chicago Press, 1948); I. Engnell, *Studies in Divine Kingship in the Ancient Near East* (Oxford: Basil Blackwell, 2nd edn, 1967).

2.   F. Crüsemann, *Der Widerstand gegen das Königtum* (WMANT, 49; Neukirchen–Vluyn: Neukirchener Verlag, 1978); G.E. Gerbrandt, *Kingship According to the Deuteronomistic History* (SBLDS, 87; Atlanta: University Microfilms International, 1986).

3.   On the place of monarchy in the structure of the book of Judges see my *The Book of Judges*, pp. 92-118; and there more bibliography. A more specific approach, which finds an actual idealization of the Davidic dynasty, is to be found in O'Connell, *Judges*, pp. 268-304.

the one hand, various expressions used in descriptions of enthronement, and in the stories and prophecies of the book, reveal the high status of the king and a concept of kingship like that of the other cultures of the ancient Near East. On the other hand, there is a marked tendency to disparage the king's status and detract from the glory of royalty.

First let us see how the book extols the virtues and high status of kingship. Here are four points by way of illustration:

1. The king is elected and anointed by God; the election and the act of anointing endow him with a special sanctity. God chose Saul (1 Sam. 9–10) and later David and his descendants (1 Sam. 16; 2 Sam. 7). Saul is described as 'ruler over his own people' (1 Sam. 10.1), his sacred status being revealed in, for example, David's response to Abishai's suggestion to attack Saul: 'Don't do him violence! No one can lay hands on the Lord's anointed with impunity' (1 Sam. 26.9).

2. God has a special relationship with the king and his offspring. According to the vision of Nathan the prophet, this relationship is an everlasting covenant, and God himself would punish the royal house if it violated it: '...I will establish his royal throne forever...When he does wrong, I will chastise him with the rod of men and the afflictions of mortals'. The relationship between God and the king is described as that between father and son: 'I will be a father to him, and he shall be a son to Me' (2 Sam. 7.13-14).[4]

3. The king, endowed with a spark of divine wisdom, is responsible for justice in his kingdom: 'And David executed true justice among all his people' (2 Sam. 8.15). His ability to judge justly derives from this special grace, he is having, as the wise woman of Tekoa put it, 'My lord is as wise as an angel of God, and he knows all that goes on in the land' (2 Sam. 14.20).[5]

4. The stories in the book of Samuel also stress the king's place and position in the religious ritual. He builds a temple to God and possibly also serves in it as priest. David offered sacrifices

4.   The description of the king as the son of God—which also occurs in Ps. 2; 1 Chron. 17.13; 22.10; 28.6—raised the scholars' interest in the issue of deification of the king, but this lies outside the present study.

5.   See also 1 Kgs 3.

to God when the ark was brought to Jerusalem (2 Sam. 6.14-
18), and it is stated: 'and David's sons were priests' (2 Sam.
8.18b).[6]

Yet despite these references to the king's exalted status and his connection to God, the book of Samuel depicts the monarchy as a flesh-
and-blood institution, as far from divinity as earth is from heaven, and
there is no attempt to disguise its defects. The description of the reason
for establishing the monarchy already shows this, as do the characters
of the kings and their actions described throughout the book:

1. The appointment of a king is shown as an initiative of the
    people, not of God. The elders of Israel appealed to Samuel to
    set a king over them. God's responds by saying, 'it is me they
    have rejected as their king' (1 Sam. 8.7b). The preference for
    a flesh-and-blood kingship, then, is interpreted as a rejection
    of divine rule. Nevertheless, God instructs Samuel to give the
    people a king, and at the same time to warn them against him:
    'Heed their demand; but warn them solemnly, and tell them
    about the practices of any king who will rule over them'
    (1 Sam. 8.9). God accedes to the people's demand to appoint
    a king, but asks Samuel to inform them about the negative
    aspects of monarchy. And still the people insist: 'But the peo-
    ple would not listen to Samuel's warning. "No", they said.
    "We must have a king over us, that we may be like all the
    other nations: Let our king rule over us, and go out at our head
    and fight our battles"' (vv. 19-20). The monarchy is therefore
    an expression of the people's will, rather than God's. In one
    way or another, it is imposed upon God.
2. The characters of the individual kings are not depicted as per-
    fect either. The first king, Saul, failed to obey God's com-
    mand: '…for you have rejected the Lord's command, and the
    Lord has rejected you as king over Israel' (1 Sam. 15.26b). As
    a result, the monarchy was taken away from his family. The
    second king, David, failed morally (he committed adultery,
    had one of his officers murdered and took his wife for himself)
    and was punished, in that his posterity would never know

---

6.   The chronicler discarded this information, which did not fit the law of the
Torah, and according to his version, 'David's sons were first ministers of the king'
(1 Chron. 18.17b).

peace: 'the sword shall never depart from your House' (2 Sam. 12.10).

3. Royal rule did not prevent upheavals, such as Saul's forays against David in the midst of the struggle with the Philistines; in David's reign there were two uprisings which shook the kingdom, that of Absalom and that of Sheba son of Bichri. These uprisings suggest that there was unrest and dissatisfaction with the king's rule.

In summary, we see that side by side with the influence of the ancient Near Eastern cultures, which emphasized the link between the king and the deity, there is in the book of Samuel a marked tendency to denigrate the monarchy. This no doubt expresses an ideology of depreciating the king's status and pointing out the gulf between the single almighty God and the king, who is mere man. The fact that the book devotes so much attention to the failings of the kings, rather than to their achievements, exposes the limitation of monarchy and its predominantly negative aspects. For sheer quantity alone, it is significant that while more than twenty chapters (including the first two chapters in 1 Kings) are devoted to the reign of David, the greatest king of Israel, only six (2 Sam. 5–10), that is, less than a third, relate his achievements. Most of the description concerning either Saul or David exposes the king's human weaknesses and failures.

No less significant is the aspect of combination, namely, the author's literary devices that serve to depreciate the kings. In the book of Samuel the figure of the prophet is given a superior status as the intermediary between God and the king, thereby emphasizing the latter's distance from God.

In the historical reality it is reasonable to assume that the position of the kings of Israel was no less exalted than that of other kings in the ancient world, and prophets posed no threat to their power. But since the author of the book of Samuel was not a courtier, he could permit himself to write from a prophetic viewpoint, and compose a history wherein the power of kings was circumscribed by prophets.

This tendentious account of history begins as early as Saul's rise to power. In Samuel's farewell speech (1 Sam. 12), having chastised the people for the evil deed of demanding a king, the prophet concludes with the words, 'As for me, far be it from me to sin against the Lord and refrain from praying for you; and I will continue to instruct you in the practice of what is good and right... For if you persist in your wrongdoing, both you and your king shall be swept away' (1 Sam. 12.23-25). Here Samuel and God are depicted as occupying one side of the equation, with the king and the people on the other side. The king is merely the first among equals, and both he and his people need a prophet to mediate between them and God. The prophet is thus depicted as standing higher than the king, and this hierarchical view is maintained throughout the book. The prophet is shown as the king-maker. It is the prophet who chooses Saul to be king (1 Sam. 9–11), and he who informs him that the throne is taken away from his house (1 Sam. 13; 15), anoints David as the new king (1 Sam. 16), determines who will build the temple (2 Sam. 7), admonishes David about the Bathsheba affair, and determines the future of his kingdom (2 Sam. 11–12 in relation to the subsequent narrative: ch. 13 to 1 Kgs 2). The king is depicted as dependent upon the prophet and chastised by him, while the prophet appears on God's behalf. His prophecies are fulfilled and he knows what is going to happen—as Second Isaiah puts it, 'See, the things once predicted have come, and now I foretell new things, announce to you ere they sprout up' (Isa. 42.9). The book of Samuel, with its emphasis on the role of the prophet and of prophecy, may therefore be described as prophetic historiography, on which Alexander Rofé pointed out, 'Prophetic historiography, as opposed to general historiography, characteristically offers a causal explanation of events in the "word" of the prophet, either as a vision of the future or as a doctrine and admonition'.[7] Indeed, there are many prophetic admonitions and fulfilled prophecies throughout the book. Samuel prophesies to Saul what will happen to him on his way home (1 Sam. 10.1-8), and the narrator confirms, 'and all those signs were fulfilled that same day' (v. 9b); he also prophesies to Saul about the fate of his royal house before the battle of Michmash and after the war with the Amalekites (1 Sam. 13; 15). Finally, he reveals to Saul, through the woman with the 'familiar spirits' in Endor, the outcome of the forthcoming battle in Mount Gilboa (1 Sam. 28). The life of David is likewise accompanied by prophecies, from his secret anointing by Samuel in Bethlehem to Nathan's admonition, which predicts and describes all that would befall his house and his kingdom: 'Therefore the sword shall never depart

7.   A. Rofé, *The Prophetical Stories: The Narratives about the Prophets in the Hebrew Bible, their Literary Types and History* (Jerusalem: Magnes Press, 1986 [Heb.]), p. 71. Rofé thinks that the prophetical historiography came later than the beginning of writing history in the tenth century BCE.

from your House—because you spurned me by taking the wife of Uriah the Hittite and making her your wife'; and further: 'even the child also to be born to you shall die' (2 Sam. 12.1-14). And indeed, the sequel of events shows both prophecies being fulfilled.

All this may create the impression that the prophet replaces God in the book of Samuel, but this is not the case! The author takes pains to include stories which reveal the prophet's weaknesses and his being a messenger who is utterly dependent on his sender. One example is the story of Samuel's arrival at Bethlehem to anoint David as the next king (1 Sam. 16). The author makes it plain that the seer did not know who the candidate was and kept making mistakes. Seeing Eliab he said, 'Surely the Lord's anointed stands before Him', but God tells him ironically, 'Pay no attention to his appearance or his stature, for I have rejected him. For not as man sees; man sees only what is visible, but the Lord sees into the heart' (1 Sam. 16.6-7). The prophet makes the same error seven times, with each of Jesse's sons, until finally he asks, 'Are these all the boys you have?', thus showing that he is unaware that there is another young boy who is out with the sheep. When David is brought before him, God says to Samuel, 'Rise and anoint him, for this is the one' (1 Sam. 16.11-12). The limits of the prophet's knowledge and his dependence on his sender could not have been illustrated more vividly than by this episode.

The important contribution that the book of Samuel makes to biblical historiography may be summed up by two points, an ideological one and a poetical one. Ideologically, the book makes it clear that the king of Israel is not an omnipotent absolute monarch, a step away from divinity, but, rather, a human figure who is liable to sin and fail as humans do. It is the prophet who stands above him, who appoints him, transmits God's wishes to him and reproves him when he goes wrong. The prophet is an authority vis-à-vis the king, but in himself is a mere messenger.

The second contribution, linked to the first, has to do with the writing of history. By setting the prophet above the king the author demonstrates the non-courtly nature of the narrative and stresses that it is a prophetic historiography.

The next chapter discusses the philosophical world-view of the Deuteronomist authors, that is to say, the composers of historiography based on the philosophy of the book of Deuteronomy, and examines its links to the prophetic historiography.

Chapter 5

THE BOOK OF DEUTERONOMY AS A SOURCE OF IDEOLOGY

The previous chapter dealt with the book of Samuel and its central idea, namely, the concept of monarchy. We saw that the formation of the Israelite monarchy took place in the shadow of the prophecy that presented the encounter between king and prophet as a contest between earthly needs versus sublime principles, and subjected both the king and the course of history to those principles.

An examination of another historiographic book that deals with the monarchy, namely, the book of Kings, reveals its relation to those principles. At the same time, it introduces other principles of which there is no trace in the book of Samuel, and which show a marked link to the book of Deuteronomy. This chapter is devoted to Deuteronomy, which is a major nexus in the evolution of biblical historiography, both in its central ideas and their distinctive expression.[1]

On the face of it, the book of Deuteronomy—also called Mishneh Torah, which means, 'a copy of the law'—recapitulates the substance of the previous books of the Pentateuch. In reality it is an independent and distinctive segment of it.[2] The book is introduced as Moses' farewell speech in which he summarizes the past, but in fact it is a separate entity. It repeats such phrases as 'this Teaching', 'this book', 'this book of Teaching' (as one example out of many see Deut. 28.58-61), which indicate that it regards itself as an independent work. Certainly none of the other component parts of the Pentateuch is described as a book. The differences become discernible as one looks closer. The book of

1. On the time, ideas and style of Deuteronomy, see G. von Rad, *Studies in Deuteronomy* (SBT, 9; trans. D. Stalker; London: SCM Press, 1963); M. Weinfeld, *Deuteronomy and the Deuteronomic School* (Oxford: Clarendon Press, 1972). See also critical interpretations to the book of Deuteronomy and introductions to the Old Testaments.

2. See Chapter 2, pp. 29-33.

Deuteronomy also differs from the other books of the Pentateuch in its historical description and its laws. For example, in the book of Exodus the suggestion to appoint judges is attributed to Jethro, while in Deuteronomy the stranger Jethro is not mentioned and the initiative is attributed to Moses (cf. Exod. 18 with Deut. 1.9-18). In the other books of the Pentateuch there is no restriction on the places of worship, it is otherwise in Deuteronomy.[3] Similarly, Deuteronomy includes laws of which there is no mention in the others, including the law of the king (Deut. 17.14-20), laws of war (Deut. 20), and so on. Thus there is no doubt that this is a separate book, and one of the main questions concerning it is when it was composed.

Probably no other biblical book has been dated by scholars with such unanimity as the book of Deuteronomy. As early as 1805 the German scholar de Wette pointed out the connection between it and Josiah's religious reform.[4] Since then it has been the widespread conviction of researchers that the book preceded the reform—which means that it dates from the seventh century BCE—and served as its ideological platform. The book of Kings describes the centralizing reform of worship carried out by Josiah, following the finding of a book in the repairing of the temple (2 Kgs 22-23). And indeed Deuteronomy is the only book of the Pentateuch which decrees that religious worship must take place in one place, and bans all others. This centralization of worship lies at the very heart of Deuteronomy, the manifesto of a new ideology which criticized the former beliefs and opinions that had been held sacred for hundreds of years. I can start a short summary of the central tenets of this ideology with the concept of God.

The book of Deuteronomy stresses the monotheistic idea, and even contends with the question of the existence of other gods. Accordingly, the people of Israel realized that 'the Lord alone is God; there is none else beside him...he Lord alone is God in heaven above and on earth below; there is no other' (Deut. 4.35-39). As for other faiths, such as the worship of the sun, the moon or the stars, the same chapter affirms that 'These the Lord your God allotted to other peoples everywhere under heaven' (Deut. 4.19), meaning that the worship of other gods, of

---

3.   A few examples will suffice: Gen. 12.7-8; 13.18; Exod. 20.24; in contrast to Deut. 12.

4.   See Chapter 2 n. 20.

the heavenly bodies and the various national deities, and so on, also exists by God's might and at his will.[5]

The book of Deuteronomy also opposes any concrete conceptions of the deity. It attacks anthropomorphism—that is, the personification of God in human form—and insists that the image of God is an unknown. Here the book introduces its own version of the events on Mount Sinai, according to which the people heard the voice of God but did not see his image (Deut. 4.10-20), and this is given as the reason for the ban on making graven images: 'For your own sake, therefore, be most care-ful—since you saw no shape when the Lord your God spoke to you at Horeb out of the fire—not to act wickedly and make for yourselves a sculptured image in any likeness whatever: the form of a man or a woman...' (vv. 15-16). Whereas in Exodus the text makes it clear that God came down from heaven and was present on Mount Sinai (Exod. 19.18-24), in Deuteronomy only his voice is heard from the fire. The physical proximity of God is replaced in Deuteronomy by emotional proximity, by his responding to every appeal of Israel: 'For what great nation is there that has a god so close at hand as is the Lord our God whenever we call upon Him?' (Deut. 4.7).[6]

This new concept of God, distancing him from human and leaving him in the heaven, led to a new approach to divine worship. Deuteron-omy insists that the temple is the place that God has chosen to install his name. In contrast to popular belief and priestly opinion that God actually resides in the temple, the Deuteronomist maintains that it is only God's name which resides therein, whereas God himself is in heaven. This view has several implications. Thus, for example, in Deut-eronomy the ark is no longer God's seat, but merely a wooden box con-taining the tablets of the law. Similarly, the sacrifices are not held to be 'the food of God' (Lev. 21.6, 8, 17, 21, 22, 25), as the priestly belief maintained, and God has no need of the 'pleasing odour' (Exod. 29.18, 25, 41, etc.) of the burnt offerings. According to Deuteronomy, the sacrifices are chiefly the 'peace offerings' that are eaten in the temple by those who make them, a rite that serves both a social purpose of

---

5.   On the time of ch. 4, its chronological strata and its place in Deuteronomy, see A.D.H. Mayes, 'Deuteronomy 4 and the Literary Criticism of Deuteronomy', *JBL* 100 (1981), pp. 23-51; A. Rofé, 'The Monotheistic Argumentation in Deut-eronomy IV 32-40: Contents, Composition and Text', *VT* 35 (1985), pp. 434-45.

6.   See Weinfeld, *Deuteronomy*, pp. 191-209; and von Rad, *Deuteronomy*, pp. 38-39; and the bibliography mentioned there.

feeding the needy and the worshipper's desire to express his feelings
for God. In keeping with this view, the religious rituals in Deuteronomy
are accompanied by prayers, confessions and thanksgiving, and the
depiction of the ritual makes almost no reference to its technical aspects
and the role of the priests.

The Deuteronomistic revolution, stemming from a different concept
of God, his abode and the demands he makes on human beings, was
accompanied by a series of actual everyday acts, the principal of which
was the centralization of worship. No more numerous temples and high
places—henceforth there was to be a single temple, established by
Josiah in Jerusalem. This temple was cleared of all features which might
hint at the worship of other deities, or at a concrete, tangible concept of
the God of Israel. Apparently the centralization also made it easier to
supervise this matter. It is possible to deal with the social and economic
implications of this centralism, while the present study deals only
with its religious significance. Yet the demand for a centralized worship
affected all the ritual laws (Deut. 12; 14; 15.19-23), the holy days
(Deut. 16.1-17), the gifts to the priests (Deut. 18.1-8; 26.1-10), and
even the civil judiciary (Deut. 16.18–17.13; 19). It may be said that the
way of life of the Israelite individual was profoundly affected by this
process, as two specific illustrations reveal: the centralization meant
that ordinary animal slaughter became profane, since it is unlikely that
the slaughtering of all meat for food was carried out at the one temple
(Deut. 12.15-28); secondly, it changed the manner in which the
religious festivals were celebrated—the Passover sacrifice, for example,
turned from a family sacrifice into a public one at the central temple
(Deut. 16.1-8).[7]

So far we have dealt with the concept of the deity and religious worship, but Deuteronomy also had distinct views regarding the relations
between God, the people and the land. Accordingly, the people are
redefined: having been chosen to worship God, the Children of Israel
are taken out of 'the iron furnace' of Egypt to be God's 'people of
inheritance' (Deut. 4.20). The choice is arbitrary, having nothing to
do with the quantity or quality of the people, but only with the love of
God and his oath to their forefathers (Deut. 7.7-8; 9.4-5). The choice
renders the people sacred—meaning, set apart—and this sanctity entails

7.   All these issues are discussed in the critical commentaries on the book of
Deuteronomy.

a separation from the other nations and their customs (Deut. 7.6; 14.2, 21). The demand to keep apart has many implications regarding the ancient inhabitants of the land (Deut. 7; 20.16-18) and relations with strangers or others (Deut. 23.2-9). The book of Deuteronomy commands the people to distance themselves from the inhabitants of the country and from their religions, and demands that they be utterly destroyed. The sanctity applies to the people, not to the land (which is described as a reward for keeping the covenant), and so the people who inherit the land must utterly destroy the inhabitants and their places of worship. At the same time, the book makes no less extreme and explicit demands on the Israelites with regard to keeping the laws and commandments and the exclusive devotion to God (Deut. 6.7).

The lawmaker of Deuteronomy also refers to the leadership of the people and to the relations between the nation and God. The law of the king (Deut. 17.14-20) has a negative attitude towards the monarch. As in the book of Samuel, the creation of the monarchy is a result of the people's clamouring for a king, but the author of Deuteronomy stresses: 'Be sure to set as king over yourself one of your own people; you must not set a foreigner over you, one who is not your kinsman' (Deut. 17.15). The king, no less than his subjects, is obliged to keep the religious laws, which means that their status is higher than the king's. While in the book of Samuel the king and the people are equal before the prophet, in Deuteronomy they are equal before the laws: 'Let it remain with him and let him read in it all his life, so that he may learn to revere the Lord his God...Thus he will not act haughtily toward his fellows...' (vv. 19-20). Though the king is God's elected, he has no direct connection to the deity. The basis of the relations between God and his people is rooted in 'this book of the law', and all other contacts were to be held through prophets (Deut. 18.15-19). Deuteronomy thereby assigns supreme importance to the prophets, yet it is also conscious of the problems of their appearance and of distinguishing between a prophet whom God has sent and a false one who speaks 'presumptuously' in God's name (vv. 20-22).

Thus far we have discussed the central ideas in the book of Deuteronomy. Let us now look at its form. According to Moshe Weinfeld, who devoted much of his research to the book of Deuteronomy and the Deuteronomistic school,[8]

---

8. See n. 1 above.

The seventh century BCE marked a turning-point in the history of literary creativity in Israel. The latter half of that century saw the rise of a novel and distinctive literary style which would pervade almost the entire Israelite literary output during the following 150 years (650–500 BCE). The style makes its first appearance in the book of Deuteronomy...From here it passed to the historical books and the prophetic literature (particularly that of Jeremiah). It is characterized by simplicity, fluidity and clarity. It has typical turns of speech, notably a rhetorical quality. The chief characteristic of the phrases in Deuteronomy is not necessarily their use of new idioms, since many of these may be found in older sources...Rather, the Deuteronomistic innovation is expressed in a... distinctive jargon which reflects the religious transition of that period.[9]

According to Weinfeld, 'What makes a phrase deuteronomic is not its mere occurrence in Deuteronomy, but its meaning within the framework of Deuteronomic theology', and he stresses that the Deuteronomistic idioms revolve around theological themes such as the singularity of God and the struggle against polytheism, the centralization of worship, the keeping of the statutes and the covenant, and all the principles mentioned above.[10] By way of illustration, here are some of the phrases that are considered typical of the Deuteronomistic style. The centre of worship is called 'the site where the Lord your God will choose'; God does not reside there, but chooses 'to establish his name there'. The inclusion of the poor in the ritual sacrifice is phrased thus: 'you and your sons and your daughters, your male and your female slaves, and the Levite in your settlements'. The inclusion of the Levites among the deprived is characteristic only of Deuteronomy. The following phrase recurs in reference to the conquest of the land: 'you defeat them, you must doom them to destruction: grant them no terms and give them no quarter' (Deut. 7.2). The commandment to worship God is put in these explicit and emphatic words: 'you shall love the Lord your God with all your heart and with all your soul and with all your might' (Deut. 6.5). This clear, detailed style undoubtedly served to underline the very particular ideology of the book of Deuteronomy.

9.   M. Weinfeld, *From Joshua to Josiah: Turning Points in the History of Israel from the Conquest of the Land until the Fall of Judah* (Jerusalem: Magnes Press, 1992 [Heb.]), p. 180.

10.   See Weinfeld, *Deuteronomy*, pp. 1-2 and Appendix A (Deuteronomic phraseology, which is classified thematically), pp. 320-59.

When we compare the books of Judges and Samuel with Deuteronomy, we find that they contain some of its ideas. Thus the book of Judges emphasizes that doing evil in the eyes of the Lord is the cause of the people's historical destiny. The book of Samuel stresses the negative aspects of monarchy and the mediating role of prophecy. Nevertheless, many of the core ideas of the Deuteronomistic philosophy are missing in these books, despite the existence of a context for mentioning them—for example, the centralization of worship, the transcendent concept of God, the place of 'this Teaching' or 'this book of Teaching', and so on. Moreover, they are not characterized by the language and style devised by the Deuteronomic school. That is why I believe that they were written earlier than the book of Deuteronomy, and that they influenced its composition. In any event, once the book of Deuteronomy appeared, it influenced the writing and shaping of the later historiographic books, those which are commonly styled the Deuteronomistic books.

The next chapter will examine the characteristics of a Deuteronomistic historiographic book, that is to say, an account of history that reflects the world-view of the book of Deuteronomy.

Chapter 6

DEUTERONOMISTIC HISTORIOGRAPHY

The previous chapter outlined the central ideas of the book of Deuteronomy, because these ideas shaped some of the historiographical books in the Bible. Let us begin with the book of Kings, which is most obviously related to Deuteronomy and its teaching.[1]

Reading the book of Kings one gains the impression that it is based on archival sources, as the following concluding statements suggest: 'The other events of Rehoboam's reign, and all his actions, are recorded in the Annals of the Kings of Judah' (1 Kgs 14.29); or: 'The other events of Ahab's reign, and all his actions—the ivory palace that he built and all the towns that he fortified—are all recorded in the Annals of the Kings of Israel' (1 Kgs 22.39), and elsewhere. Those books of chronicles must have been accounts of the most important acts of the kings and their outstanding characteristics—namely, their wisdom or bravery, their major building enterprises, wars and so forth.[2] To us, the significance of these statements lies in the suggestion that the book of Kings contains only parts of the material in those chronicles, and the question arises as to what the author chose to include and what he left

1. Critical scholars agree that 'the spirit of the editor is fully Deuteronomistic'. Quoted from J.A. Montgomery, *The Books of Kings* (ICC; New York: Charles Scribner's Sons, 1951), p. 45; see also there n. 3. They are divided on questions such as how many layers of compilation are to be found, and where and when was most of the editing done. See S.L. McKenzie, *The Trouble with Kings: The Composition of the Book of Kings in the Deuteronomistic History* (VTSup, 42; Leiden: E.J. Brill, 1991).

2. The annals belong to the royal archives. The editor also made use of temple archives (see, e.g., 1 Kgs 6; 7; 8.1-13, 62-64), oral traditions such as the stories of the prophets (as, e.g., the Elijah and Elisha cycles), editorial orations (2 Kgs 17.7-23; 21.11-16; and more), and even fictional tales like the story of Naboth's vineyard (1 Kgs 21, with comparison to 2 Kgs 9.25-26).

out. Clearly, the sources being unavailable, we have no way of knowing what he chose to omit, but there are enough clues to suggest that
among the omissions were acts of bravery and building enterprises
which would have redounded to the king's credit. For instance, all we
know about Ahab's ivory palace and the cities he fortified is comprised
in these brief hints; the only specific mention in the book of Kings
refers to the temple of Baal, which he built in Samaria (1 Kgs 16.32).
However, the extant book of Kings reveals what elements were chosen
for inclusion, so that all in all the reader can deduce the aim of the book
of Kings in its extant form.

Looking back, it may be said that the historian responsible for the
book of Kings sought to explain what caused the downfall of the kingdoms of Judah and Israel. This is why he wrote their histories syn-
chronously, side by side, with the emphasis on the sins of their kings,
which he interpreted as responsible for the destruction of both kingdoms.

A systematic examination of the text shows that the criteria and
principles guiding the author's view of the conduct of the different
kings, and his judgment that they sinned, were derived from the ideology of the book of Deuteronomy. The book of Kings contributes to this
ideology by applying it to the history of the First Temple period and by
adding substantial details. The historical concretization is especially
marked with reference to two subjects: the House of David and Jerusalem. When the author of Kings refers to the site chosen by God 'to
establish his name there'—a recurring phrase in Deuteronomy[3]—he
does not mean any site in any of the tribal lands, but very specifically
Jerusalem: 'Jerusalem—the city where I have chosen to establish my
name' (1 Kgs 11.36).[4] Likewise, when he speaks of a royal house
which God chose and with which he made an eternal covenant, he is
referring to the dynasty of David, the monarch described in the book of
Kings as the model of obedience to God's commandments and statutes.
Only once does the author of Kings concede that David sinned, and
even then, only after praising David, saying that he 'had done what was
pleasing to the Lord and never turned throughout his life from all that
he had commanded him'; nevertheless he adds: 'except in the matter of
Uriah the Hittite' (1 Kgs 15.5). This remark suggests that the Deuteronomistic editor of Kings is at odds with the book of Samuel. As he

3. See Deut. 12.5, 11, 21; 14.23, 24; 16.2, 6, 11; 26.2.
4. Cf. 1 Kgs 14.21.

sees it, the murder of Uriah is not so heinous a deed as the author of the book of Samuel suggests. The author of Kings chooses to depict David as God's favourite. The book of Deuteronomy, which consists largely of laws given by Moses in the wilderness, deliberately avoids, in many cases, any reference to later historical events and both Jerusalem and the house of David are not mentioned. By contrast, these historical references carry particular weight in the book of Kings. In this way, the book of Kings serves as a historical commentary to the book of Deuteronomy, defining the temple built by Solomon in Jerusalem as God's chosen place, and David's dynasty as God's chosen royal house.

These associations between the books of Deuteronomy and Kings appear in another series of links that occur throughout the latter and are part and parcel of the leading ideas of the former.

Let us look first at the place and role of prophecy.[5] Prophets hold a central position in the book of Kings, embodying the idea expressed in Deuteronomy, and influenced by the important role of the prophet in the book of Samuel: 'I will raise up a prophet for them from among their own people, like yourself [Moses]: I will put my words in his mouth and he will speak to them all that I command him' (Deut. 18.18). These prophets enthrone kings—as for example, the first Jeroboam (1 Kgs 11.29-39) and Jehu, son of Nimshi (2 Kgs 9.1-13)—and chastise kings, as in the case of Elijah and Ahab (1 Kgs 21.17-27), among others. When in distress the king turns to the prophet to obtain God's response, as happened with Hezekiah during the siege of Sennacherib. He sent his ministers, 'Eliakim, who was in charge of the palace, Shebna the scribe, and the senior priests, covered with sackcloth, to the prophet Isaiah' (2 Kgs 19.1-7; the quotation is from v. 2).

The author of Kings is greatly concerned with the confrontation between king and prophet and with the latter's miraculous powers.[6] One of the miracle stories that illustrates this concern is that of Naaman's leprosy. Naaman, the commander of the army of the king of Aram, who

---

5.   See Chapter 4, n. 7.

6.   Both motifs appeared previously in the book of Samuel, though in different proportions. In Samuel the emphasis was on the confrontation between the king and the prophet (Saul–Samuel, David–Nathan), and less on the prophet's miraculous deeds (exceptional cases being 1 Sam. 7; 12.18-19; 2 Sam. 24.11-19). In the book of Kings the emphasis is upon the prophets' miraculous deeds, as shown by the various stories. This is especially true of the prophet Isaiah, who, but for the book of Kings, would not have been known as a miracle-worker.

was afflicted with leprosy, heard from a captive Israelite girl who served his wife that there was in Samaria a prophet who could cure him. He appealed to his king, who passed his request to the king of Israel. When the king of Israel heard this he tore his clothes and said: 'Am I God, to deal death or give life, that this fellow writes to me to cure a man of leprosy? Just see for yourselves that he is seeking a pretext against me' (2 Kgs 5.7). Thus, he implies that the king of Israel suspects the king of Aram of looking for an excuse to attack him, and admits that anyone who can cure leprosy is godlike. When Elisha the man of God heard about the reaction of the king of Israel, he sent to tell him the following: 'Why have you rent your clothes? Let him come to me, and he will learn that there is a prophet in Israel' (2 Kgs 5.8). This subtle story depicts the prophet as almost equal to God, possessing powers that give him an advantage over the kings and captains of this world.[7]

All through the book of Kings there are prophets whose prophecies are fulfilled and create a cyclic effect.[8] Quite early in the book there is a story about a man of God who came to Jeroboam, son of Nebat, as he was about to burn incense in Beth-El and, addressing the altar, said: 'O altar, altar! Thus said the Lord: A son shall be born to the House of David, Josiah by name; and he shall slaughter upon you the priests of the shrines who bring offerings upon you. And human bones shall be burned upon you' (1 Kgs 13.2). And indeed all these things came true in the reign of Josiah—namely, towards the end of the book (2 Kgs 23.15-16).[9] Moreover, throughout the book there are such phrases as: 'in accordance with the word that the Lord had spoken through his servant the prophet Ahijah' (1 Kgs 14.18); or, 'just as the Lord had spoken through Elijah' (2 Kgs 1.17), and many more. This is the author's reaffirmation that history is but a fulfilment of prophecies.

The connection between the book of Kings and Deuteronomy is obvious in other ways too, such as the insistence on the universal concept of God. The story of Naaman's leprosy is one example. Once

---

7. An analysis that concentrates on the poetics of this story is to be found in Y. Zakovitch, *'Every High Official Has a Higher One Set over Him': A Literary Analysis of II Kings 5* (Tel Aviv: Am Oved Publishers, 1985 [Heb.]).

8. See von Rad, *Deuteronomy*, pp. 74-91; Rofé, *The Prophetical Stories*, pp. 85-91.

9. The LXX version emphasizes the connection between the prophecy and its fulfilment.

cured of his ailment, Naaman is not content only to thank and reward
the prophet, but utters a monotheistic declaration, 'Now I know that
there is no God in the whole world except in Israel!' (2 Kgs 5.15), and
undertakes hereafter to worship YHWH, for which purpose he carries
away a load of earth from the land of Israel. He goes so far as to beg the
prophet's forgiveness if in future he is obliged by his position at his
king's side to take part in alien cults and rituals.

This is not an exceptional declaration in the book of Kings. Solomon's prayer at the dedication of the temple opens as follows: 'O Lord
God of Israel, in the heavens above and on the earth below there is no
god like you' (1 Kgs 8.23a). He then proceeds to describe the temple as
a place of worship for all men, including strangers and all the people of
the earth (1 Kgs 8.38-43).[10]

In the chapter that dealt with the book of Deuteronomy I stressed that
the acknowledgment of the God of Israel as the one and the only deity
is coupled with a demand for exclusive devotion to YHWH and an absolute prohibition against worshipping any other gods. In the book of
Kings this demand becomes a criterion for judging the kings. Solomon
is charged that in his old age, his wives turned away his heart after
other gods, and that 'he was not wholeheartedly devoted to the Lord his
God, as his father David has been. Solomon followed Ashtoreth the
goddess of the Phoenicians, and Milcom, the abomination of the Ammonites. Solomon did what was displeasing to the Lord and did not
remain loyal to the Lord like his father David. At that time, Solomon
built a shrine for Chemosh and he did the same for all his foreign wives
who offered and sacrificed to their gods' (1 Kgs 11.4-8). This accusa-
tion is used by the editor to explain the breakup of the kingdom. That
was the reason, he states, that God decided to split the united kingdom
into two: Israel and Judah (1 Kgs 11.11-13).[11]

Another example is the book of Kings' sweeping denunciation of
King Ahab, son of Omri, king of Israel. Ahab must have been a power-
ful king who did a great deal to the kingdom's international standing
and strengthen its inner cohesion. By means of shrewd marriage ties he
cemented alliances with the Phoenicians in the north and Judah in the

10. It seems that the phrase 'among all your people Israel' in v. 38 is a late
addition, as certain manuscripts of the LXX show; and see also J. Gray, *I & II Kings*
(OTL; London: SCM Press, 3rd edn, 1977), p. 225.

11. Cf. 1 Kgs 11.29-39 and pay attention to the fact that in the LXX, the Vulgate
and other versions, v. 33 is phrased in the singular and the subject is Solomon.

south.[12] He is also described as a builder, namely, fortifier, of cities.[13] The Assyrian annals for the reign of Shalmaneser the Third, king of Assyria (858–824 BCE), show Ahab as a member of an anti-Assyrian alliance, which included many of the kingdoms of the region.[14] However, these close ties with the kings of the regions exposed Israel to alien cultural influences, as shown, inter alia, by Ahab's building a temple to Baal served by the Baal priests. As a result, he is execrated by the author of Kings as the one who 'did more to vex the Lord, the God of Israel, than all the kings of Israel who preceded him' (1 Kgs 16.33b). Ahab's reign is the backdrop for Elijah's bitter struggle against the worship of Baal, as well as a yardstick for measuring sin. The book's author compares Manasseh to Ahab, signifying that Ahab's reign was a major factor in God's decision to exile Israel: 'I will apply to Jerusalem the measuring line of Samaria and the weights of the House of Ahab; I will wipe Jerusalem clean as one wipes a dish and turns it upside down' (2 Kgs 21.13).

A contrasting example is, of course, Hezekiah, king of Judah. This king, evidently a political chancer, dared to rebel against Assyria and brought Judah to the brink of disaster. During his reign Assyria conquered a large part of Judah, destroyed many cities and exiled their inhabitants, and even laid siege to Jerusalem.[15] Following the campaign of Sennacherib, king of Assyria, Judah paid heavy tribute and the kingdom was economically devastated, but the sudden lifting of the siege crowned Hezekiah with eternal glory. The author of the historical account in the book of Kings ignores the devastation of Judah in Hezekiah's reign. He interprets the lifting of the siege as a sign from

12. As well as taking the Phoenician Jezebel as his wife, daughter of king Ethbaal of Sidon (1 Kgs 16.31), he married his own daughter Athaliah to Joram, son of Jehoshaphat, king of Judah (2 Kgs 8.18, 26-27; 2 Chron. 18.1).

13. See 1 Kgs 22.39. It is interesting to see how the Deuteronomist turns the building and fortification of Jericho, in Ahab's case, into a pejorative account (1 Kgs 16.34; cf. Josh. 6.26). And see Gray, *Kings*, pp. 369-71. The ivory tablets found in Samaria, the stables at Megiddo (layer IV), and the findings in Hazor (layer VIII), testify to his building enterprises.

14. In the sixth year to the reign of Shalmaneser the Third (853 BCE), according to the Monolith Inscription from Kurkh, Ahab the Israelite was an important partner in a coalition that fought against assyria in Karkar. See *ANET*, pp. 278-79.

15. The Bible is not the sole source of information on these events. There are also Assyrian sources, and on some points—as for example, tax gatherers—they correspond to the biblical account to a remarkable degree. See *ANET*, pp. 287-88.

God predicted by the prophet Isaiah (2 Kgs 19.20-35), and describes
Hezekiah as carrying out a religious reform and being the greatest of
the kings of Judah (2 Kgs 18.4-6),[16] well worthy of divine liberation.

So much for the depiction of kings in accordance with the principle
of devotion to God, and the manner in which their actions were judged
and evaluated. One of the significant measures was the adoption of another major Deuteronomistic principle, namely, the centralization of the
worship. The book of Kings points out that the first steps of centralization were carried out in the reign of Hezekiah (2 Kgs 18.4) and especially under Josiah (2 Kgs 22.3–23.20). There is no detailed description
of the reform in connection with Hezekiah, and it is difficult to gauge
its extent; some scholars maintain that Hezekiah is credited with religious reform because he saved Jerusalem.[17] By contrast, the account of
Josiah's reign describes how a book was found whose contents were
affirmed by Huldah the prophetess, and that following the book and its
confirmation Josiah carried out an extensive reform of the religious ritual. He purified the temple and defiled high places and other shrines.
Then he celebrated Passover in the temple, and as the author of the
book of Kings notes: 'Now the passover sacrifice had not been offered
in that manner in the days of the chieftains who ruled Israel, or during
the days of the kings of Israel and the kings of Judah. Only in the eigh-
teenth year of king Josiah was such a passover sacrifice offered in that
manner to the Lord in Jerusalem' (2 Kgs 23.22-23). There is no doubt
that these actions conformed with the spirit of Deuteronomy. As noted
in the previous chapter, the family sacrifice was replaced by a public
one in the chosen location. According to the editor of the book of
Kings, these changes took place only in the reign of Josiah.

Furthermore, the entire book of Kings is marked by an apologetic
tone regarding the many altars. Feeling impelled to explain why in the
time of Solomon the people were able to sacrifice in the high places,
and Solomon himself sacrificed in the great high place in Gibeon, the
author adds: 'The people, however, continued to offer sacrifices at the
open shrines, because up to that time no house had been built for the

16. On the assumptions about this reform, see Chapter 2 n. 17. See also Weinfeld, *From Joshua to Josiah*, pp. 156-62. Many researchers have learned about this
reform from the Chronicler (2 Chron. 29–31), without questioning his reliability.

17. See Chapter 2 n. 17.

name of the Lord' (1 Kgs 3.2). With the temple in Jerusalem standing, the issue of the high places becomes a criterion for judging the kings. Thus, for example, Asa, king of Judah, excelled in purifying the ritual, yet even about him it is said: 'The shrines, indeed, were not abolished; however, Asa was wholehearted with the Lord his God all his life' (1 Kgs 15.14-15). In fact, the determined effort to end the worship in the high places was made in Josiah's reign, which is why this king is so highly esteemed: 'There was no king like before who turned back to the Lord with all his heart and soul and might, in full accord with the Teaching of Moses; nor did any like him arise after him' (2 Kgs 23.25). Thus the issue of centralized worship was a criterion for judging all the kings of Judah.

We have also seen that Deuteronomy prohibits any physical concept of God. This principle serves the author of Kings when he condemns the places of worship in Dan and Beth-El, above all because in these places Jeroboam set two golden calves that he presented as the god of Israel: 'This is your god, O Israel, who brought you up from the land of Egypt! That proved to be a cause of guilt' (1 Kgs 12.28-30).

By contrast, the author makes Solomon utter a liturgical speech in which he states that the temple is not God's abode: 'But will God really dwell on earth? Even the heavens to their uttermost reaches cannot contain you, how much less this house that I have built!' (1 Kgs 8.27). The speech proceeds to emphasize the importance of the house as a place of prayer and supplication.

The case of Hezekiah, who merits a special commendation in the book, is particularly interesting. It is said that 'He trusted only in the Lord the God of Israel; there was none like him among all the kings of Judah after him, nor among those before him. He clung to the Lord; he did not turn away from following him, but kept the commandments that the Lord had given to Moses' (2 Kgs 18.5-6). We find that he merited this commendation because he not only removed high places, broke up the images, and cut down the cultic object Asherah, but 'He also broke into pieces the bronze serpent that Moses had made, for until that time the Israelites had been offering sacrifices to it; it was called Nehushtan' (2 Kgs 18.4). Thus I learn in passing that the Israelites went on sacrificing offerings to the bronze serpent even in the days of David and Solomon. This shows that through most of the First Temple period the Israelite religion was still syncretistic, containing elements of pagan

worship, including the worship of concrete objects like the bronze serpent.[18]

We may therefore conclude that the book of Kings is inspired by the
theological principles of the book of Deuteronomy. The departure from
these principles explains the downfall of Israel and Judah. Though we
have not listed all these principles, enough has been pointed out to
reveal the close relationship between the two books, and how the history of the First Temple period served as a proving-ground for the
Deuteronomistic ideology.

The next chapter will deal with other texts in which the beliefs and
opinions of Deuteronomy may be found.

18. An important illumination of the way Israel worshipped God may be found,
e.g. in the archaeological findings at Khirbet el-Kom and Kuntillet 'Ajrud. See J.A.
Emerton, 'New Light on Israelite Religion: The Implications of the Inscriptions
from Kuntillet 'Ajrud', *ZAW* 94.1 (1982), pp. 2-20.

Chapter 7

THE CONQUEST OF THE LAND: HISTORY OR IDEOLOGY?

The last chapter was devoted to the book of Kings, which deals with the history of Israel and Judah during the First Temple period. In this chapter I shall examine a central event set in an earlier period, the conquest of the land as described in the book of Joshua, and I shall follow this with its association with Deuteronomistic ideology.

According to the book of Joshua, the country was conquered in a single military campaign led by Joshua, the disciple of Moses, and with the participation of all the Israelite tribes. The process of the conquest is described systematically and in logical order. It begins with the preparations for the conquest, including the organization of the army, the dispatch of spies, the crossing of the Jordan river, the renewal of the precepts of circumcision and the celebration of Passover by way of spiritual preparation, culminating in the appearance of God's messenger, to remind Joshua that the war to be fought is the war of God too (Josh. 1–5). Only then do Joshua and the people launch the war, which may be divided into three stages. In the first stage they conquer some cities in the central region. The first city to fall is Jericho (Josh. 6), followed by Ai (Josh. 7–8), with the result that the cities of the Gibeonites, headed by Gibeon itself—a big, strong city inhabited by warriors—prefer to surrender and avoid war (Josh. 9). In the second stage they overcome the Amorite alliance of the five kings, led by Adonizedec, king of Jerusalem. This victory completes their control of the south of the country (Josh. 10). In the third stage they fight against the alliance of the kings of the north, headed by Jabin, king of Hazor, and occupy the north of the country (Josh. 11). Thus the entire land is conquered, a large number of its inhabitants are killed, and what is left is to be apportioned to the tribes.

But a comparison between this narrative and the archaeological findings, in sites whose identification is unmistakable, reveals a total discrepancy that casts doubts on the historical reliability of the book of

Joshua's description of the conquest. It should be noted that biblical scholars began to doubt the Joshua narrative as far back as the late nineteenth century, prompted by contradictions in the book of Joshua itself and its comparison with the book of Judges.[1] Nowadays the researchers are convinced that the destruction of the Canaanite cities was a process that lasted over 100 years. Thus, for example, Hazor was destroyed in the middle of the thirteenth century BCE, whereas Lachish was destroyed towards the end of the twelfth century BCE. Moreover, the archaeological evidence shows that the cities of Jericho, Ai, Hebron and others were not even inhabited on the eve of the tribal settlement. It is therefore unlikely that there was a single campaign, led by a single commander, in the course of which the aforesaid cities were conquered.[2] In fact, the most recent archaeological exploration has largely borne out the conclusion of Alt, who argued that the settlement of the Israelites was not a process of conquest but a gradual settlement by nomads, who moved from the desert and its fringes into unoccupied grazing lands in the inhabited land.[3] Indeed, in the late 1960s following the Six-Days War, when it became possible for Israeli archaeologists to explore the central mountain region, they discovered hundreds of settlements that came into being during the twelfth and eleventh centuries BCE in areas which had previously been uninhabited or very thinly populated.[4] No wonder, then, that the current state of archaeological evidence has produced a general consensus among biblical researchers and historians of Israelite history in biblical times regarding the conquest of the land and its settlement. The accepted description is that the Canaanite civilization collapsed in a process that culminated in the

1.   See Wellhausen, *Prolegomena*, pp. 441-48; G.F. Moore, *Judges* (ICC; Edinburgh: T. & T. Clark, 1966 [1895]), pp. 3-10 (bibliography, p. 3). The case of Hebron will serve as an example: the tradition in Josh. 11.21-23, according to which Joshua is the conqueror, differs from Josh. 15.13-19; 14.6-14; Judg. 1.11-15 and Judg. 1.10, 20.

2.   N. Na'aman, 'The "Conquest of Canaan" in Joshua and in History', in N. Na'aman and I. Finkelstein (eds.), *From Nomadism to Monarchy: Archaeological and Historical Aspects of Early Israel* (Jerusalem: Yad Izhak Ben-Zvi, The Israel Exploration Society, 1990 [Heb.]), pp. 284-347.

3.   A. Alt, 'The Settlement of the Israelites in Palestine', in *idem, Essays on Old Testament History and Religion* (trans. R.A. Wilson; Garden City, NY: Doubleday, 1966 [1925]), pp. 175-221.

4.   I. Finkelstein, *The Archaeology of the Israelite Settlement* (Jerusalem: The Israel Exploration Society, 1988).

middle of the twelfth century, parallelled with a slow process of settlement which began in the central mountain region on both sides of the Jordan, as well as the Galilee, and only later spread to the Judaean mountains, the plains and the Negev.

But if the settlement was a slow process, rather than a sweeping conquest by a well-organized social group led by a single leader, what are we to make of the narrative in the book of Joshua? In light of the new data, the story of the conquest as told in that book is not a depiction of a historical reality, but a literary fiction whose purpose we may legitimately examine. Did it represent a particular ideology, and if so, who was behind it, when was it written and for what purpose?

To answer this question, let us briefly examine the story of the Gibeonites (Josh. 9). According to this narrative, the Gibeonites, one of the Hivite group of Canaanite peoples inhabiting four cities in the Land of Benjamin, disguised themselves as coming from a far country, in order to deceive Joshua and the Israelites and persuade them to strike an alliance with them rather than attack them. The Israelites were taken in, and being persuaded that this was not a local nation, struck an alliance with the Gibeonites. When the deception was uncovered the Israelites could not undo the oath they had sworn to the Gibeonites, and were therefore barred from destroying and exterminating them and could not treat them as they treated the other inhabitants of the land. Nevertheless, they refused to overlook the deception and condemned the Gibeonites to be hewers of wood and drawers of water for the altar of the Lord.

There is no doubt that the plot of this narrative, the dialogues in it and its end, which ties the Gibeonites to 'the place which he should choose' (9.27), reveal its profound connection to the Deuteronomistic ideology. The laws of war in Deuteronomy (ch. 20) distinguish between the inhabitants of 'all towns that lie very far from you' and of 'towns that belong to nations hereabout' (Deut. 20.15). The writer specifies: 'In the towns of the later peoples, however, which the Lord your God is giving you as a heritage, you shall not let a soul remain alive. No, you must proscribe them...lest they lead you into doing all the abhorrent things that they have done for their gods and you stand guilty before the Lord your God' (Deut. 20.16-18). The Gibeonite deception is therefore based on their knowledge of the Deuteronomic law. To escape the penalty of destruction, the Gibeonites, one of the nations of the land, disguised themselves as visitors from a far-off land, with whom it was permitted to strike an alliance on terms of surrender. This event is therefore recounted in the book of Joshua by way of the exception that proves the rule. The Gibeonites are described as an exceptional case of survival that underlines the other cases of total conquest in accordance with the law of destruction, a Deuteronomic law.[5]

Shmuel Ahituv, in his book *Joshua: Introduction and Commentary*, raises the question, 'How much historical substance is there in the story of the Gibeonites?' His own answer is that

> most of the Gibeonites were exterminated by Saul (2 Sam. 21), and their territory was seized by the Benjamites. The Gibeonites, inhabitants of the Hivite enclave in the inheritance of Benjamin, were one of the Canaanite remnants left among the Israelites. There were other such enclaves in Israel until their conquest by David and the absorption of their populations among the Israelites…The presence of the Gibeonites in their cities must be viewed against the background of the Israelite settlement in the country, in the process of which not all the local inhabitants were destroyed…The settlement of the Israelites occurred in a number of ways, and in this case evidently in peaceful ways which were probably not spoilt until the reign of Saul.[6]

Ahituv is pointing to the discrepancy between the historical core and the later narrative. The historical core of the story is the presence of a Hivite enclave in the territory of Benjamin, which survived even after its persecution by Saul, and was associated with the worship in the temple of Gibeon mentioned in the reign of Solomon (1 Kgs 3.4-5).

A similar discrepancy is evident with regard to the conquest. The historical core is the gradual collapse of the power of the Canaanite cities in favour of a new entity which arose in the region during the thirteenth to eleventh centuries BCE. On the other hand, the description in the book of Joshua, according to which Joshua and the Israelites were the faithful executors of the Deuteronomic laws of war, is an ideological description that gives the story of the conquest a Deuteronomistic character.

5.   J. Blenkinsopp, 'Are There Traces of the Gibeonite Covenant in Deuteronomy?', *CBQ* 28 (1966), pp. 207-13; P.J. Kearney, 'The Role of the Gibeonites in the Deuteronomic History', *CBQ* 35 (1973), pp. 1-19.

6.   S. Ahituv, *Joshua: Introduction and Commentary* (Mikra Leyisra'el; Tel Aviv: Am Oved Publishers; Jerusalem: Magnes Press, 1995 [Heb.]), pp. 155-56.

So far we have answered only one part of the question. We have found that the narrative of the conquest in the book of Joshua represents the Deuteronomistic ideology, which propounded the law of Herem, which is utter destruction. We have yet to answer the second part of the question, namely, what was the purpose of the Deuteronomistic school in describing a ruthless conquest in accordance with the law of Herem? Why was it necessary to depict Joshua as a conqueror who left nothing standing, who destroyed and did not spare a single soul? Before answering this question, let me point out that the book of Joshua itself acknowledges the existence of many remnants and that the law of Herem was not fully carried out, as stated in 13.2: '...and very much of the land still remains to be taken possession of'. And there is Joshua's own reference to 'these nations that still remain' or 'these nations that are left among you' (23.4, 7). Similarly, the books of Judges, Samuel and Kings refer to the Canaanite population living side by side with the Israelites. Thus Uriah the Hittite served in David's army, and Solomon's building projects were made possible largely thanks to the 'tribute of bondservice' which he levied upon 'All the people that were left of the Amorites, Hittites, Perizzites, Hivites, and Jebusites, who were not of the Israelite stock' (1 Kgs 9.20-21). It appears that historical reality is one thing and a history composed according to ideological principles is something else. In the historical reality groups of various origins, which may be designated by the general name proto-Israelites, settled in the mountain regions and gradually formed ties of mutual cooperation. Moreover, certain sociological and anthropological theories, which lie beyond the scope of this discussion, suggest that some of these settlers were remnants of Canaanite society and nomadic groups that lives on its margins (according to such scholars as Mendenhall,[7] Gottwald[8] and Finkelstein[9]). In any event, when the Canaanite cities crumbled and some of their inhabitants became nomads, a new economic pressure was exerted on the population of the periphery and was followed by a process of settlement in all parts of the country. Only when these marginal elements grew stronger, during the reigns of Saul and David, did they struggle for dominance in the region,

7.   G.E. Mendenhall, 'The Hebrew Conquest of Palestine', *BA* 25 (1962), pp. 66-87.

8.   N.K. Gottwald, *The Tribes of Yahweh* (Maryknoll, NY: Orbis Books, 1979).

9.   Finkelstein, *Israelite Settlement*.

defined their identity as Israelites, and by degrees sought to give their state a distinctive character of its own.

Why, then, with the rise of the Deuteronomistic school in the seventh century BCE, was the ideology of the Herem developed and a depiction of the conquest composed that was a purely literary construct, quite detached from the historical reality it supposedly described? The answer to this question is closely related to the religious-cultural revolution which swept Judaean society after the exile of the northern Israelite kingdom (at the end of the eighth century BCE).[10] Judaean society, or at any rate its intellectual members, wanted to understand why the threat of destruction and exile hung over them, what must be done and how they must conduct themselves if they wished to avoid the fate of the Israelite kingdom and its inhabitants. They even wondered about Hezekiah's merits, thanks to which Jerusalem was spared in his reign. The search for answers to these and similar questions led them to conclude that the source of the trouble lay in their abandonment of their God and the penetration of alien cultural influences, and that the highest merit was the exclusive worship of the God of Israel. The cultural assimilation, a direct result of the Assyrian policy of exile, led them to the theoretical conclusion that had their environment been free from alien influences, and had the people remained faithful to their God, history might have been different. This gave rise to the law of Herem, which distinguished between the near and the far away, and to the idea that violating the law—namely, sparing the Canaanites—would leave the Israelites vulnerable to undesirable cultural influences. It was therefore permissible to strike alliances with remote nations, but not with the Gibeonites who lived in their midst. Above all, it was necessary to avoid the pernicious influence of the adjacent cultures, encountered on a daily basis.

These conclusions, illustrated by means of a historical narrative, came to have a decisive impact upon both present and future. The need to keep apart from the nations became a factor which enabled the society to survive and maintain its independent being in conditions of exile. Furthermore, keeping apart became a guiding principle in the national life of the returnees from Babylonian exile in their relations with the population that had remained in the country and that surrounded them. The careful cultivation of the identity of the 'holy seed' as against the

10. Y. Amit, 'Teaching the Book of Joshua and its Problems' (Heb.), *Al Haperek* 2 (Jerusalem: The Ministry of Education and Culture, 1986), pp. 16-22.

'abominations' of 'the peoples of the lands' (Ezra 9.1-2) was a natural continuation of the Deuteronomistic ideology. Ezra's narrative concerning the mixing of the holy seed among the nations of the lands, among whom he mentions the Canaanite, the Hittite, the Perizzites, the Jebusites and the Amorites, who had all vanished long before, recapitulates the terrible error of the period of the conquest. In other words, the description of the conquest in the book of Joshua, while supposedly relating to the past, was by way of a moral lesson and a warning to future generations and to the returnees, who were in a sense the new conquerors, telling them what they must avoid and how they must act, so that the people would live in peace and security in their land. In this way, the Deuteronomistic ideology uses the description of the past as a guide to the present and moral precepts for the future.

We may therefore conclude that the Herem law could not have been applicable in the time of the conquest, since it was a lengthy process of settlement and other political-social changes; nor, for that matter, was it applicable during the Persian period, in the time of the returnees, since by then there was not a trace left of the old Canaanite nations. But the existence of the law as an ideological principle instructed the exiles and returnees how to preserve their cultural distinction.

It should be noted that the theme of the conquest of the land is only one of several indications of a close link between the book of Joshua and Deuteronomy. Such subjects as the inheritance of the land,[11] references to the book of the Torah or the Law of Moses,[12] the demand to cleave to God, to love and fear him at all times,[13] and other themes which have not been mentioned here and which likewise echo the style of Deuteronomy,[14] all indicate that the story of the conquest in the book of Joshua was devised in the spirit of the ideology of the book of Deuteronomy.[15]

---

11. Josh. 1.11, 13, 15; 12.6, 7; 21.42; 22.4; 23.1, 3, 4, 5, 9, 12, 13, 15, 16.

12. Josh. 1.7, 8; 8.31, 32; 22.3, 5; 23.6.

13. Josh. 4.24; 22.3, 5; 23.4, 8, 11.

14. For example, the monotheistic creed (Josh. 2.11), retribution and punishment (Josh. 1.7; 23.13, 15, 16).

15. See the various critical commentaries on the book of Joshua, as well as various introductions to biblical literature. The traces of Deuternomistic redaction are especially noticeable in Josh. 1–12; 22.1-8; 23. The Priestly redaction of this text (13–21; and 22.9-34) is not dealt with here.

So far we have looked at two books which reflect the philosophical world of Deuteronomy—namely, the book of Joshua—in the context of the conquest—which follows it in the biblical sequence, and Kings, which concludes the Deuteronomistic narrative.[16] Set between these two, which represent the rigid Deuteronomistic framework, are the books of Judges and Samuel, which, though not such unequivocal expressions of the philosophy of Deuteronomy, do contain, as I have shown, some of its incipient ideas. Consequently, the author of the Deuteronomistic history felt free to include them in his extensive composition.[17]

This author used a number of different sources, including existing writings, archival documents, chronicles and various traditions, some of which he included verbatim and others he adapted to fit his work. But sometimes the assemblage and editing were insufficient, and then the author and his school wrote fresh material. The story of the Gibeonites is a case in point. Even if the historical memory retained some information about the destruction of the Gibeonites in the reign of Saul (2 Sam. 21), or the shrine at Gibeon in the reign of Solomon (1 Kgs 3.4), the story of their surrender in the book of Joshua was a new one, and its basic plot is obviously Deuteronomistic. In this way, the great Deuteronomistic composition includes new writings, responding to the needs of the ideology of the book of Deuteronomy. The narrative of the conquest of the land must be one such work.

The next chapter will deal with the four former books of the Torah and not only with Deuteronomy.

16. See Chapter 6.

17. On the different view of the great Deuteronomistic composition, held by many scholars, see Chapter 2, pp. 29-33.

Chapter 8

GENESIS TO NUMBERS: AS PROCESSED BY PRIESTLY IDEOLOGY

The previous chapters dealt with Deuteronomy, with the historiographic works that influenced it (the books of Judges and Samuel) and
those that were influenced by it (the books of Joshua and Kings). We
have seen that this body of literature covers the period from the exodus
from Egypt to the destruction of the First Temple. I pointed out that not
all the books were written by the Deuteronomistic author; however,
they were probably edited to make them fit into this ideological framework, which may be called 'Prophetic Historiography', on account of
the central role played in it by prophets and their prophecies.

What, then, is the place of the other books of the Pentateuch, from
Genesis to Numbers? Critical biblical research in the nineteenth century
already distinguished between the Pentateuchal sources comprised in
these books: the Yahwist, marked J; the Elohist, marked E; the Priestly,
marked P, and a part of it marked H; and the book of Deuteronomy,
which was seen as a separate and independent source and marked D.[1]
Martin Noth, who has already emphasized the role, scope and significance of Deuteronomistic historiography, also argued that the great
Deuteronomistic composition should be set apart from the four books
that precede it (Genesis, Exodus, Leviticus and Numbers), which deal
mainly with the gradual emergence of the nation from the time of the
Patriarchs to the end of the wanderings in the wilderness, that is, to the
conquest of Canaan.[2] The present study is concerned with the common
philosophy or ideology that unites these books and differs them from
that of Deuteronomy. Let us recapitulate some of the central ideas
characterizing the Deuteronomistic composition, to see if they conform

1. Further discussion of these sources may be found in all critical introductions
to the Bible. A popular and thrilling presentation of this scholarly approach is to be
found in R.E. Friedman, *Who Wrote the Bible?* (New York: Summit Books, 1987).
2. See Chapter 2 n. 22; Noth, *The Deuteronomistic History*.

to the accounts of Genesis through to Numbers, and to what extent they resemble the ideology reflected in these books. But first we must ask to what extent the period described in these books can be discussed in terms of credible history, since it is known that the less an account adheres to history the more likely it is to be tendentious.

Critical research has been increasingly sceptical about the historical credibility of the narratives from Genesis through to Numbers. Modern researchers tend to view the historical picture arising from these texts as primarily a national myth charged with ideals and moral meaning.[3] Thus the binding of Isaac must not be treated as a historical event, but as a moral tale designed to move history, according to Gunkel, or to direct history, according to Auerbach.[4] Many of the scholars reached this conclusion when they despaired of finding any historical evidence for many elements of the world depicted in these stories, and consequently turned their attention to such questions as the date of their composition, the ideological circles responsible for their creation, and the like.[5]

3.   This trend began in classical critical research at the end of the nineteenth century. Thus, for example, Wellhausen (*Prolegomena*) interpreted the stories of the Pentateuch as reflections of later periods. On the other hand, Hermann Gunkel, in the introduction to his commentary on Genesis (H. Gunkel, *The Legends of Genesis: The Biblical Saga and History* [trans. W.H. Carruth; New York: Schocken Books, 1964]), emphasized the difference between history writing and the legendary character of the Genesis stories: 'History...claims to inform us what has actually happened...while legend is by nature poetry, its aim being to please, to elevate, to inspire and to move' (p. 10).

4.   See E. Auerbach, 'Odysseus' Scar', in *idem*, *Mimesis: The Representation of Reality in Western Literature* (Princeton, NJ: Princeton University Press, 1953 [German orig. 1946]), pp. 3-23. According to Auerbach: 'The story of Abraham and Isaac is not better established than the story of Odysseus, Penelope, and Eurycles; both are legendary. But the biblical narrator, the Elohist, had to believe in the objective truth of the story of Abraham's sacrifice—the existence of the sacred ordinances of life rested upon the truth of this and similar stories' (p. 14).

5.   To mention only a few prominent studies: T.L. Thompson, *The Historicity of the Patriarchal Narratives* (BZAW, 133; Berlin: W. de Gruyter, 1974); *idem*, *The Origin Tradition of Ancient Israel* (Sheffield: JSOT Press, 1987); *idem*, *Early History of the Israelite People: From the Written and Archaeological Sources* (Leiden: E.J. Brill, 1992); J. Van Seters, *Abraham in History and Tradition* (New Haven: Yale University Press, 1975); N.P. Lemche, *Early Israel: Anthropological and Historical Studies on the Israelite Society before the Monarch* (VTSup, 37;

Here are a only few examples taken from the mentioned studies showing that the accounts in these books are not historically credible.

The tales of the Patriarchs include references to the Philistines, the Hivites and Hittites as being among the inhabitants of the country. However, the historical evidence shows that these particular ethnic groups arrived in Canaan in the early Iron Age, that is to say, after the settlement of the Israelite tribes, so that their presence in the time of the Patriarchs cannot be sustained.

Furthermore, there is no evidence for the existence of such sites as Beersheba and Hebron—both of which figure prominently in the geographical range of the stories of the Patriarchs—during the Late Bronze Age, but again, only from a later time, after the settlement.

Nor is there any evidence in Egyptian literature, with its continuous written record, of any mass exodus from Egypt. The stele of King Merenptah, dating from 1208 BCE, is the only Egyptian inscription which mentions the name Israel, closing the list of the Egyptian king's victories in his Canaanite campaign. It says: 'Israel is desolated/its seed is not'. While this is a significant reference with regard to the settlement, it tells us nothing about the exodus. Moreover, an examination of the exodus story itself raises doubts about its historicity. It is enough, at this juncture, to mention the unrealistic number of the departing Israelites, of whom 600,000 were men. This means that, together with their families, the Israelites numbered some two million—a completely untenable figure in the geographic and economic conditions of the Sinai peninsula, and could only have served to underline the signs and miracles of God's might.

These examples, among many others exposing the contradictions, discrepancies, anachronisms, resemblance to mythological and folk motifs and the like in the Pentateuchal history, illustrate the difficulty of substantiating the historical background of this literature. Therefore, let us set aside the historical problem and concentrate on the ideology, the issues relating to the tendentious nature of the narrative sequence in the first four Pentateuchal books, and its divergence from the book of Deuteronomy and the ideology it inspired.

The sequence from Genesis to Numbers famously describes the Patriarchal period (the book of Genesis), depicts the Exodus from Egypt (the first third of the book of Exodus), and deals extensively with the

Leiden: E.J. Brill, 1985); R.N. Whybray, *The Making of the Pentateuch* (JSOTSup, 53; Sheffield: Sheffield Academic Press, 1987).

wandering in the wilderness, which is also the background for the giving of the laws (the rest of Exodus through Numbers). Now, the book of Deuteronomy does make reference to the Patriarchs, but only in a formulaic manner, as 'The Lord swore to your fathers, Abraham, Isaac and Jacob',[6] without mentioning details or specific events of that period. By contrast, Deuteronomy treats the Exodus from Egypt and the wanderings in the desert as formative events, though without devoting much space to their description. There is enough of it, however, to enable us to compare it with the account in the other Pentateuchal books and to draw conclusions from the differences.

Thus, in the first four books Moses does not act alone; his brother Aaron is his right-hand man, and in the course of the narrative is made the head of a priestly dynasty, as spelled out in the laws concerning the tabernacle: 'You shall bring forward your brother Aaron, with his sons, from among the Israelites, to serve me as priests...They shall make those sacral vestments for your brother Aaron and his sons, for priestly service to Me' (Exod. 28.1-4). The law of sacrifices also specifies that only Aaron and his sons may sacrifice to God. Moreover, an examination of the laws given to Israel in the desert in the books of Exodus, Leviticus and Numbers, reveals that most of them have to do with the tabernacle and the priesthood. Little wonder, then, that researchers have argued that scribes from the priestly school were responsible for depicting the emergence of the nation in the first four books of the Pentateuch. This is the place to point out that priests, their functions and status figure only marginally in the fifth book—Deuteronomy. By laying emphasis on a single place of worship, the book of Deuteronomy undermined the priesthood, leaving large numbers of them redundant without temples to serve in; this accounts for the lower status of the Levites in the book of Deuteronomy: 'And you shall rejoice before the Lord your God with your sons and daughters and with your male and female slaves, along with the Levite in your settlements, for he has no territorial allotment among you' (Deut. 12.12).[7] The Deuteronomic legislation virtually ignores many of the religious rites. In other words, the philosophical world of the Deuteronomic school differed in its attitude towards the ritual procedures from the work that gave pride of

6. Deut. 1.8; cf. vv. 21, 35; 4.31, 37; 6.3; 8.1; 11.9, 21; and more. Most references relate to the motif of the promise. The reference in 26.5 is exceptional, and its generalized use of laconic form has given rise to various interpretations.
7. Cf. Deut. 12.18-19; 14.27-29; 16.11, 14; 26.11-13.

place to the tabernacle, its structure, rites and the priests who served in
it.

In the books of Exodus through to Numbers, Moses has a unique role
to play and, unlike Deuteronomy, in these books prophecy does not appear to be an institution with a future.[8] The priesthood, by contrast, represents a permanent institution, responsible for the integrity and purity
of the nation. This function is expressed in the priestly apparel of
Aaron, which includes the names of the tribes of Israel engraved on
gemstones. The priest is also responsible for judging the Israelites by
means of the Urim and Thummim, among other things. It is therefore
the serving priest, rather than the prophet, who is the people's permanent representative before God.

Let us see to what extent the ideas of Genesis through to Numbers
conform with the priestly circles. I say conform, because it is not
argued that these books were written in their entirety by the priestly circles. I do maintain, however, that even those parts which were not
written by priests and which reflect ancient popular traditions (usually
ascribed to the Yahwist [= J] or Elohist [= E] sources), conformed, or at
any rate did not conflict, with the priestly world-view, and could thus
be incorporated in a composition edited by priestly circles.

Let us begin again with the concept of the deity. In these books the
concept is corporeal, and God and his angels are anthropomorphic enti-
ties.[9] God has an image (Gen. 1.26-27) and he is accompanied by
angels, who can function as messengers, and by sons of God (Gen.
3.22-24; 6.1; 18–19), and maintains a personal contact with his creatures. On special occasions they may even see him, as in the events at
Mount Sinai (Exod. 19–20) and the dedication of the tabernacle (Lev.
9.23-24). God appears 'in the cloud over the cover', which is why the
priest may not freely enter the holy place (Lev. 16.2). God's near presence accompanies the people of Israel either as a cloud, which both
guides and protects them, or as a 'glory'—that is to say, a real, concrete
presence, physically close to its worshippers, and not a remote, abstract
entity. This is how it is expressed: 'I will abide among the Israelites,
and I will be their God. And they shall know that I the Lord am their
God, who brought them out from the land of Egypt, that I might abide
among them, I the Lord their God' (Exod. 29.45-46); or: 'the cloud had

8.   The conditional phrasing of Num. 12.6 underlines this: 'When a prophet of
the Lord arises among you…'; KJV: 'If there be a prophet among you…'
9.   The examples are many, therefore I do not cite more than one or two.

settled upon it and the Presence of the Lord filled the tabernacle"
(Exod. 40.35). In this matter the priestly outlook resembles the popular
conceptions. It assumes that the divine entity has a permanent presence
within the ritual precinct in the midst of the people, shown by the
repeated phrase 'before the Lord', as in the following: 'Add one flat
loaf of bread, one cake of oil bread, and one wafer, from the basket of
unleavened bread that is before the Lord' (Exod. 29.23; and many other
verses). The ark inside the tabernacle is not merely a chest made of
acacia wood (Exod. 25.10-22; cf. Deut. 10.1-5). Stress is laid on its
gold overlay, the cherubim stretching their wings over it, and its function as God's abode: 'There I will meet with you, and I will impart to
you—from above the cover, from between the two cherubim that are on
top of the ark of Pact...' (Exod. 25.22). The priestly school, which
composed a creation story in which God rested from all the work that
he had done (Gen. 1-2.4a), was untroubled by a description of God
walking in the garden in the cool of the day (Gen. 3.8), and could
incorporate it into the work it edited. Its general outlook was, as noted
before, close to many popular views.

An examination of the concept of the deity reveals how much the
school which fashioned the first four Pentateuchal books differed from
the Deuteronomist school, which strove to distance itself from all expressions of anthropomorphism and corporeality, and insisted on the
remoteness of God, who could be heard but could never be seen.[10]

Inevitably, in these first four Pentateuchal books the concept of religious worship also differs from that of Deuteronomy. They ascribe an
equal degree of holiness to various locations, such as Beth-El, Hebron
and Beersheba, none preferable to the others.[11] After the war with
Amalek (Exod. 17.15) and following the giving of the Law on Mount
Sinai (Exod. 24.4-7) altars are built and sacrifices are offered. Though
there is one mobile tabernacle in the wilderness, it can be regarded as
an exigency of the nomadic life in the desert, since the priestly consti-
tution does not contain an explicit prohibtion against multiple shrines.
The subject of ritual worship occupies centre stage with meticulous
legislation, which can reveal that its primary function is to sustain the
deity and provide for his needs.

10. See Chapter 5, pp. 50-52.
11. This tendency becomes extreme in the avoidance of the mention of Jerusalem, which is the concretization of the chosen place. See Chapter 6, pp. 57-58.

This concept originates in the ritual heritage of the surrounding nations, and is referred to in the Pentateuchal stories. Thus, for example, God's promise not to unleash another deluge is described as his response to Noah's sacrifices after the flood: 'The Lord smelled the pleasing odour, and the Lord said to himself: "Never again will I doom the earth because of man"'; and so forth (Gen. 8.21). This resembles the reaction of the gods in the Mesopotamian story of the flood, which describes them as gathering like flies when they smell the sacrifices burnt by Ut-Napishtim.[12] Similarly, the priestly laws specify: 'Place all these on the palms of Aaron and his sons, and offer them as an elevation offering before the Lord. Take them from their hands and turn them into smoke upon the altar with the burnt offering, as a pleasing odour before the Lord; it is an offering by fire to the Lord' (Exod. 29.24-25). There have been various attempts to interpret these descriptions as reflecting a refinement, in that God is described as only smelling the odour rather than actually eating the burnt sacrifices, but as Licht has noted, these interpretations diverge from the plain biblical text, and cannot do away with the basic association with the ritual heritage of the region's shrines.[13] This shows that in the matter of the ritual itself the concept that characterizes the first four Pentateuchal books also differs from that of Deuteronomy and the literature it influenced.

There are also obvious differences in the view of the people and the land. The priestly school shows openness to the absorption of outside elements. The stranger could enjoy the rights of a citizen, provided he was circumcised and obeyed the ritual customs, as follows: 'If a stranger who dwells with you would offer the Passover to the Lord, all his males must be circumcised; then he shall be admitted to offer it; he shall then be as a citizen of the country. But no uncircumcised person may eat of it. There shall be one law for the citizen and for the stranger who dwells among you' (Exod. 12.48-49). A liberal attitude towards strangers is found in much of the first four books of the Pentateuch. A mixed multitude accompanied the Israelites when they came out of Egypt (Exod. 12.38), nor is there any attempt to disguise or condemn marriage with non-Israelite women, as in the case of Joseph and Asenath, the daughter of a priest of On (Gen. 41.45, 50), Moses and

12. *The Epic of Gilgamesh*, tablet 11 ll. 160-61 (*ANET*, p. 95).
13. J.S. Licht, 'Pleasing, Pleasing Odor', *Encyclopaedia Biblica*, V (Jerusalem: The Bialik Institute, 1968 [Heb.]), pp. 831-32.

Zipporah, the daughter of the priest of Midian (Exod. 2.21), and many more.

The land of Canaan is the land of God, and its inhabitants (= the Israelites) are called 'strangers resident' (Lev. 25.23). Departure from the land is a natural occurrence and not necessarily a dreadful punishment. Abraham went to Egypt after he invoked God by name, not as punishment (Gen. 12.10), and even resided in Gerar (Gen. 20); Isaac did much the same (Gen. 26.6-11); his son Jacob lived in Paddan-aram for many years (Gen. 31.41); Joseph became a great man in Egypt, and his brothers went there, driven by famine, and stayed on, enjoying the privileges granted on account of Joseph, for hundreds of years, until a king rose who knew not Joseph (Gen. 37–Exod. 1.8). The wandering in the wilderness is the formative period of the nation, during which it repeatedly provoked and tried God (Num. 14.21; practically from Exod. 14 to the end of Numbers) The wilderness is not depicted as a dreadful place—in contrast to the book of Deuteronomy, which describes it as 'the great and terrible wilderness with its seraph serpents and scorpions, a parched land with no water in it' (Deut. 8.15), and as the place where God tested his people by hardship (Deut. 8.2). In other words, life outside the national territory and marriage with foreign women are not depicted in these priestly edited books as a threat or a national fault.

The priestly editors, inspired by these concepts, created a historical narrative unlike those created by the Deuteronomistic school. Here it is shown that even in the wilderness it was possible to maintain a sacred system with the worship of God at its core. According to Wellhausen, this historical description and its inherent concepts reflect the realities of life after the downfall of the kingdom of Judah, in view of the need to cope with life in exile. In his view, the priestly literature was composed and edited in the sixth and fifth centuries BCE.[14] This would date the final editing of the Pentateuchal literature later than the great Deuteronomistic composition (seventh–sixth centuries BCE), which it completes. However, since the people responsible for it came from priestly circles, who reacted to the exile in a different way, it communicated a different ideological message.

14. Wellhausen, *Prolegomena*, pp. 15-167.

In this chapter I made no references to the heterogeneous quality of the priestly source, and the fact that it contains earlier and later materials,[15] but it seems that the main point has been made. The priestly school also employed the historical narrative as a means to an end, namely, to create a framework for the laws expressing its philosophy. In the following chapters I shall examine the ideologies which developed in the Second Temple period, in the light of the books of the Pentateuch and the Former Prophets (from Joshua to Kings), and how they influenced the subsequent writing of history.

15. See R.J. Thompson, *Moses and the Law in a Century of Criticism Since Graf* (VTSup, 19; Leiden: E.J. Brill, 1970).

Chapter 9

THE BOOK OF CHRONICLES: A RETELLING OF HISTORY?

We have seen that two ideological schools took part in forming the
historical sequence from the creation of the world to the destruction of
the First Temple—the Deuteronomist and the priestly school. The two
were not far apart in time, but differed in their world-views, and each of
them strove to communicate its particular ideological ideas via its historical composition. It would seem that the first composition to be completed was the great Deuteronomistic one, to which were subsequently
added the first four books of the Pentateuch, products of the priestly
school, whose writers expanded, completed or edited the material available to them as required. The priestly editing painstakingly linked the
compositions to make them into a continuous literary narrative. Thus,
for example, at the end of the book of Genesis, Joseph makes his
brethren take an oath: 'When God has taken notice of you, you shall
carry up my bones from here' (Gen. 50.25). And indeed it is said that
on the eve of the exodus from Egypt 'And Moses took with him the
bones of Joseph', and so forth (Exod. 13.19). Then, the end of the book
of Joshua affirms that 'The bones of Joseph, which the Israelite brought
up from Egypt, were buried at Shechem, in the piece of ground which
Jacob had bought for hundred kesitahs from the children of Hamor,
Shechem's father, and which had become a heritage of the Josephites'
(Josh. 24.32; see also Gen. 33.19). The verbal subordination of the text
in Joshua to the text of Genesis and Exodus reveals an editorial presence and a wish to tighten the links between the books of the Pentateuch and the Former Prophets and make them into one historiographic
sequence. It appears that once the editorial effort was complete and the
historical sequence was standing, this literary creation became the primary text of Second Temple Judaism, and further compositions that
were written referred to it in various ways. Sometimes various people
preached it or interpreted it, others were interested in rewriting sections

of it. There were others that shortened it, criticized it, ignored its contents or altered them.

The great historiographical and canonical composition that was written during the Second Temple period exemplifies these various approaches and techniques. Let us therefore proceed to the book of Chronicles, which is hardly ever read, on the assumption that it merely recapitulates the historical texts, so that for many it will be something of a discovery.

Indeed, on the face of it, the book of Chronicles does recount history from the beginning of humanity to the destruction of the First Temple and the Babylonian exile. In fact, it summarizes the entire period from Adam to King Saul in the first nine chapters, by means of genealogical name lists (Adam, Seth, Enosh, and so on; X begot Y, etc.). These lists are the preamble to the history of the house of David and the First Temple period, culminating in the downfall of the kingdom and the start of Persian rule. The ending of the book, with its reference to 'the rise of the Persian kingdom' (2 Chron. 36.20), shows that the author knew about the end of the Babylonian exile and the reign of Cyrus king of Persia (2 Chron. 36.22).[1] This suggests that it was written under Persian rule, and indeed most researchers believe that it was written in the fourth century BCE.[2] This chronological conclusion justifies the question, what prompted the Chronicler to recapitulate the history of the periods which had already been covered by the rich and extensive literature, that is the books of Samuel and kings? Moreover, a comparison between the book of Chronicles and its sources reveals that the author relied extensively on the sources we are familiar with, namely, Genesis through to 2 Kings, especially 2 Samuel and Kings, which served as the frame and main infrastructure for his work. Hence, all the more reason to find out what the Chronicler sought to add or to illuminate beyond the material given in his sources.

1. The concluding verses of the book (vv. 22-23) repeat the proclamation of Cyrus, which opens the book of Ezra. Some commentators hold that it was copied from the latter, and I have therefore left it out.

2. The Jewish tradition ascribes it to Ezra and Nehemiah (*b. B. Bat.* 15a), namely, to the latter half of the fifth century BCE. Japhet (*Chronicles*, p. 24) concludes: 'On the whole, however, the most common view is the middle one, with many scholars placing the book's composition some time in the fourth century BCE or towards its end'.

Here, too, we find the answer in ideology, though this time we are on firmer ground with more solid evidence, precisely because the book of Chronicles is so closely attached to its sources. This enables us to draw comparisons and to discern where the Chronicler remained faithful to his sources, where he ignored them or added to them, where he altered them and how—that is, by cutting or expanding, changing the contents or their sequence—and, finally, where he introduced passages written by himself. Such an examination, combined with an attempt to explain the changes and not merely note them, must study the author's methods, namely, his poetics, as well as his aims and his ideology. Here are some examples.

The historical description in the book of Chronicles is distinguished by the absence of a coherent account of the history of the northern kingdom of Israel. The author's reliance on the book of Kings, which is characterized by a synchronous account of both the kingdoms of Judah and Israel, makes his selective approach in narrating methodically only the history of the kingdom of Judah, quite obvious. He does not ignore the kingdom of Israel, but refers to it mainly where the two kingdoms interacted[3]—for example, the events related to the splitting of the kingdom in the reign of Rehoboam and the establishing of the northern kingdom by Jeroboam (2 Chron. 10–11),[4] or the relations between Jehoshaphat, king of Judah, with Ahab, the king of Israel (2 Chron. 18).[5] This tells us that in Chronicles the northern kingdom figures only marginally; there is even an obvious attempt to depict the kingdom of Judah as the home of a large portion of the northern population. For example, following the uprising of Jeroboam and the splitting of the kingdom, Rehoboam summoned the people of Judah and Benjamin to

3.   Cf. S. Japhet, *The Ideology of the Book of Chronicles and its Place in Biblical Thought* (trans. A. Barber; Frankfurt am Main: Peter Lang, 1989 [Heb. edn 1977]). Japhet emphasizes: 'Whenever the book of Kings describes some sort of contact between the two kingdoms, Chronicles transmits the episode in full' (p. 311).

4.   This episode is also mentioned in the exhortation speech of Abijah on Mount Zemaraim (2 Chron. 13.4-12), before the battle between Abijah, king of Judah, and Jeroboam, king of Israel. Further details about this event appear later in the text.

5.   The Chronicler criticizes the connections with the House of Omri. Thus, after Jehoshaphat joined Ahab in the war at Ramoth-gilead (2 Chron. 19.2), in the description of the ship-building with Ahaziah, king of Israel (2 Chron. 20.35-37), and mainly in the description of the period of Jehoram, son of Jehoshaphat (2 Chron. 21).

make war on Israel. According to the book of Kings, the war encompassed 'all the House of Judah and Benjamin and the rest of the people' (1 Kgs 12.23), whereas according to the Chronicler, the war involved 'all Israel in Judah and Benjamin' (2 Chron. 11.3)—suggesting that the author interprets the phrase 'the rest of the people' to mean 'all Israel', implying that even after the split of the kingdom into Judah and Israel, 'all Israel' dwelt in Judah, making the northern kingdom appear like a marginal entity.[6] This implication becomes explicit in a speech attributed by the Chronicler to Abijah, the son of Rehoboam, before going to war against Jeroboam (2 Chron. 13.4-12). According to this speech, the people of the northern kingdom were a handful of rogues who worshipped golden calves and were seeking to exploit the fact that 'Rehoboam was inexperienced and fainthearted and could not stand up to them' (2 Chron. 13.7).

But the historical account of the kingdom of Judah does not adhere closely to the sources of the Chronicler either. The author expands and fills in the descriptions of the 'good' kings, like David, Solomon, Jehoshaphat and Hezekiah, and relatively condenses the histories of the other kings. Moreover, he leaves out events which could mar the image of the king he wishes to present, even when they appear in his sources, or else he adapts the old description but inserts different changes in order to make it fit his ideology. The reader who is familiar with the stories of David in the book of Samuel soon perceives that the description of his reign in Chronicles is highly tendentious, as the author lifts whole portions from his sources while systematically suppressing any information that might cast David in a bad light. A good part of the account in Samuel is missing here: there are no descriptions of David's conflict with the house of Saul (1 Sam. 16–2 Sam. 4); of David's sin with Bathsheba and its consequences (2 Sam. 11–12); of the uprisings led by David's son Absalom and by Sheba, the son of Bichri, and the long struggle over the inheritance of the throne (2 Sam. 13–20; 1 Kgs 1–2). On the other hand, the book of Chronicles attributes to David a whole series of preparations for building the temple, and its subsequent organization and maintenance (1 Chron. 22–29). Indeed, it goes so far as to make Solomon appear as though he had only to carry out his father's testament. The author also ignores the sin of the high places

6. See Japhet, *Ideology*, pp. 273-74.

that Solomon built for foreign gods (1 Kgs 11), and his marrying foreign women—in brief, everything that might reflect badly on him. It is
difficult not to conclude that the book of Chronicles represents a systematic effort to cast a positive light on David, who set up and strengthened the united kingdom, and on his son Solomon, the builder of the
temple.

On the other hand, Manasseh, whom the book of Kings describes as
the greatest sinner, is depicted in Chronicles as having some positive
qualities. In Kings, Manasseh was the last straw, the one who caused
God to resolve to bring about the destruction of Judah:

> Therefore the Lord spoke through his servants the prophets: 'Because
> King Manasseh of Judah has done these abhorrent things—he has out-
> done in wickedness all that the Amorites did before his time—and be-
> cause he led Judah to sin with his fetishes, assuredly, thus said the Lord
> God of Israel: I am going to bring such a disaster on Jerusalem and
> Judah that both ears of everyone who hears about it will tingle... More-
> over, Manasseh put so many innocent persons to death that he filled
> Jerusalem [with blood] from end to end—besides the sin he committed
> in causing Judah to do what was displeasing to the Lord' (2 Kgs 21.10-
> 16).

But if in the book of Kings Manasseh is the epitome of evil, in the book
of Chronicles he is like the Cushite that changed his skin. Here there
is no trace of the above-quoted prophetic speech, and instead there
appears a description of punishment and repentance. The sinful Manasseh is taken captive by the Assyrian army, carried to Babylon, and
there realizes that he must change his ways:

> In his distress, he entreated the Lord his God and humbled himself
> greatly before the God of his fathers. he prayed to him, and He granted
> his prayer, heard his plea, and returned him to Jerusalem to his kingdom.
> Then Manasseh knew that the Lord alone was God...and commanded
> the people of Judah to worship the Lord God of Israel (2 Chron. 33.12-
> 16).[7]

----

7.   Inevitably, the scholars are divided in their interpretation of this event,
largely into three groups: those who find it reliable (E.L. Ehrlich, 'Der Aufenthalt
des Königs Manasse in Babylon', *TZ* 21 [1965], pp. 281-86); those who deny its
historicity, like Wellhausen (*Prolegomena*, pp. 226-27), who accepts it as a
Midrash; and those who take the middle road and try to discover some authentic
elements in it (Japhet, *Chronicles*, pp. 1003-1004).

These three illustrations—the relative disregard for the kingdom of Israel, the omission of the sins of David and Solomon, and the conversion of Manasseh from sinner to penitent—are sufficient, according to my opinion, to show that the author of Chronicles used his sources as he saw fit, with the result that his account of history does not resemble the account in his sources. It should be borne in mind that when he wrote, he could not have foreseen that the time would come when his work would be bound into a single canon with the other biblical books, and that our contemporaries would compare them one against the other. He probably expected his work to replace the previous ones, so that it would be read and not the others. However, by a jest of the muse of history, the book of Chronicles appears between the same covers as the previous books, and the reader can set them side by side and discover that the account of the Davidic dynasty and of the First Temple period in the books of Samuel and Kings does not match that of the book of Chronicles.

A closer look at the alterations, however petty-seeming, should reveal their ideological purpose, and how their tendency is connected with the period in which the Chronicler lived.

Both the books of Samuel and Chronicles describe David's victory over the Philistines in the battle of Baal Perazim. This is how the triumphant scene ends in the book of Samuel: 'the Philistines abandoned their idols there, and David and his men carried them off' (2 Sam. 5.21), in other words, the fleeing Philistines abandoned their idols on the battlefield, and David and his men carried them off with them as booty. In Chronicles the ending is different: 'They [the Philistines] abandoned their gods there, and David ordered this to be burned' (1 Chron. 14.12). The David of Chronicles does not carry off idols; he burns them according to the law of Deuteronomy: 'Instead, this is what you shall do to them: you shall tear down their altars, smash their pillars, cut down their sacred posts, and consign their images to the fire. For you are a people consecrated to the Lord your God', and so on (Deut. 7.5-6). The fact that the Chronicler adapted his description to meet the demands of Deuteronomy, diverging from the narrative in the source that was available to him, demonstrates the tremendous value set in his time on devout adherence to the laws of Moses.[8] Thus, in describing David, whom he is intent on depicting as a positive figure, he

8. On this subject, see T. Willi, *Die Chronik aus Auslegung* (FRLANT, 106; Göttingen: Vandenhoeck & Ruprecht, 1972).

adapts the description to the Deuteronomic statutes, making it seem that David knew them by heart and behaved accordingly.

Likewise, the book of Samuel tells us that David appointed his sons as priests: 'and David's sons were priests' (2 Sam. 8.18). But this conflicts with the statutes, which laid down that only sons of the tribe of Levi who are the descendants of Aaron might serve as priests. And so the parallel passage in Chronicles says: 'and David's sons were first ministers of the king' (1 Chron. 18.17).

The cumulative effect of such examples, whether of changes or deletions, reveals the intentions of the Chronicler, who disagreed with the account as told in his sources and saw fit to retell it in a different light. The above examples show clearly that one of his aims was to depict the people of Israel, and above all their leaders, during the First Temple period, as living in obedience to the laws of the Pentateuch.

It should be noted that his adaptation of the sources is very sophisticated and subtle, and does not always resort to omission, alteration or the insertion of new material. Sometimes he hints at his sources in order to create a new emphasis. For example, the story of the binding of Isaac in Genesis (22.1-19) tells how Abraham took his son to a mountain in the land of Moriah, without stating that this was the Temple Mount in Jerusalem.[9] It should be stressed that the phrase 'Mount Moriah' appears nowhere in Genesis, or anywhere in biblical literature, except the book of Chronicles. Here, in 2 Chron. 3.1, it is said that Solomon built the temple on Mount Moriah in Jerusalem. By means of this new, interpretative association, the author of Chronicles hints subtly at the binding of Isaac and determines that it took place in Jerusalem, on the site of the temple.[10] If we were to ask, 'What is the point of it? What did he gain by it?', the answer seems obvious enough: it invests Jerusalem with prior sanctity. In the book of Chronicles Jerusalem is not only the city of David, which he conquered fairly late in the history of Israel, but also a place that was already sanctified in the time of Abraham. No doubt this made Jerusalem seem all the holier.

9.   That is why the Samaritans have no difficulty in associating the mountain with Mount Gerizim.

10.   A close reading of this verse and its relations to 1 Chron. 21–22.1 reveals a connection with other traditions focusing on Jerusalem and Abraham. See H.G.M. Williamson, *1 and 2 Chronicles* (NCBC; Grand Rapids: Eerdmans; London: Marshall, Morgan & Scott, 1987 [1982]), pp. 203-205.

Similarly, in describing the dedication of the temple and the fire which came down on the altar, the author of Chronicles expands the account in the book of Kings, and invests the temple of Solomon with sanctity of the tabernacle which accompanied the Israelites in the wilderness. According to the Chronicler, as Solomon was dedicating the temple, fire came down from heaven and consumed the burnt offering, and the glory of the Lord filled the house, the priests could not enter, and the children of Israel saw the sight, bowed themselves and praised the Lord, 'For he is good, for his steadfast love is eternal' (2 Chron. 7.3). This description recalls the scene in Lev. 9.23-24, where the glory of the Lord filled the tabernacle and appeared to all the people, and a fire came out from before the Lord and consumed upon the altar the burnt offering, and the people fell on their faces. The resemblance between the two passages is unmistakable, as is the fact that there is no hint of this scene in the book of Kings. Quite obviously, the author of Chronicles deliberately created a parallel between the dedication of the temple and the dedication of the tabernacle in the book of Leviticus and of the altar in the book of Leviticus. By borrowing these literary motifs, he assigned the importance of the tabernacle to the temple of Solomon.[11]

The comparative method is a major tool that helps us, the latterday readers, to understand and follow the intentions of the Chronicler. But it should be kept in mind that the basis for the comparison and for finding different analogies was laid by the author himself, when he wrote his composition and created the references we have noted.

So far we have examined the close link between Chronicles and its sources which, as we have seen, were the books of the Pentateuch and avove all the Former Prophets. I have also stressed that at times he adheres closely to these works, while at other times he prefers to ignore them or change their materials. Either way, his narrative is a different historiography from the preceding, and has different aims.

Let us now try to analyse the intention behind the mass of changes made, since there can be no doubt that the author who handled his sources in such a thoroughgoing way did so with a purpose in mind.

---

11. On the importance of the temple tradition and its preference over the exodus tradition, see my article: 'The Position of the Exodus Tradition in the Book of Chronicles', in B. Uffenheimer (ed.), *Te'uda 2: Bible Studies Y.M. Grintz in Memoriam* (Heb.) (Tel Aviv: Hakibbutz Hameuchad Publishing House, 1982), pp. 139-55.

The debate about the purpose of the book of Chronicles has preoc-
cupied many scholars. At first the researchers and commentators argued
that the book reflected messianic, eschatological expectations, and was
meant to describe the salvation at the end of days.[12] They assumed that
the book was written during the Persian period, a national low point,
and therefore expressed hopes for a new and different world, hopes of
the return of the ideal kingdom of David, representing the rule of God
on earth. In other words, according to this view, the book of Chronicles
was a dream of the ideal, messianic kingdom at the end of days.

Other scholars have disagreed with this interpretation, notably Sara
Japhet in her book on the Chronicler's world of beliefs and opinions.[13]
Japhet is convinced that this is not an eschatological work—that is to
say, it is not concerned with a total change in the world,

> The primary principle underlying the book's world-view is acceptance
> of the existing world: no change to the world is anticipated in Chroni-
> cles...The world and the people are governed by fixed laws. These laws
> are a function of God's attributes as creator of the world and its ruler, a
> ruler guided by the principle of divine justice. History is one long chain
> of events, the changing manifestations of this truth...Moreover, the view
> that the natural order stems from the very nature of God, who created the
> world and rules it in absolute justice, necessitates an essentially positive,
> optimistic outlook on the world...Continuity, not change, characterizes
> the Chronistic way of thinking on every subject.[14]

Here Japhet distinguishes between eschatological literature and the literature which expresses realistic hopes of liberation and redemption,
between works concerning the end of days and the birth of a new
world, and works that reflect earthly expectations of a better future in
the real world, whose laws may be deduced from its past. The Chronicler's use of history indicates clearly that he is concerned with the
existing world. To convince his audience that the expectations he is

---

12. J.W. Rothstein and J. Hänel, *Kommentar zum ersten Buch der Chronik*
(KAT, 18; Leipzig: A. Deichert, 1927), pp. xliii-xliv; G. von Rad, *Das Geschichts-
bild des chronistischen Werkes* (Stuttgart: W. Kohlhammer, 1930), pp. 119-32.
This view was subsequently adopted by many scholars to this day.

13. Japhet, *Ideology*, pp. 493-516. She was preceded by W. Eichrodt, *Theology
of the Old Testament*, I (trans. J.A. Baker, Philadelphia: SCM Press, 1967), pp. 424-
30; W. Rudolph, *Chronikbücher* (HAT, 21; Tübingen: J.C.B. Mohr [Paul Siebeck],
1955), pp. xiii-xxiv, and through his interpretation; and others.

14. Japhet, *Ideology*, pp. 501-502.

talking about are realistic, he depicts them as real situations that pre-vailed in the national past. All he is hoping for is that history should repeat itself, and to achieve this the people of Israel must fulfil their destiny, follow the precepts of their God and be faithful to his statutes. Devotion to the ways of God would then restore the glorious times of the past.

By examining the history composed by the Chronicler we discover his hopes and strivings. In the present study, the best way to do this would be to examine a short excerpt from the book of Chronicles. I have chosen the beginning of ch. 13 in 1 Chronicles. This chapter de-scribes the bringing of the holy ark from Kirjath-Jearim to Jerusalem. According to the book of Samuel, the ark was taken to Kirjath-Jearim after the war with the Philistines in the time of Samuel (1 Sam. 4-6), and remained there throughout the reign of King Saul. When David conquered Jerusalem and set about making it his kingdom's adminis-trative and religious center, he was understandably interested in in-stalling the ark there (2 Sam. 6). But in Chronicles the story of the bringing up of the ark is preceded by the following passage (1 Chron. 13.1-5), of which there is no hint in the book of the Samuel:

> Then David consulted with the officers of the thousands and the hun-dreds, with every chief officer. David said to the entire assembly of Israel, 'If you approve, and if the Lord our God concurs, let us send far and wide to our remaining kinsmen throughout the territories of Israel, including the priests and Levites in the towns where they have pasture-lands, that they should gather together to us in order to transfer the Ark of our God to us, for throughout the days of Saul we paid no regard to it'. The entire assembly agreed to do so, for the proposal pleased all the people. David then assembled all Israel from Shihor of Egypt to Lebo-hamath, in order to bring the Ark of God from Kiriath-jearim.

In this passage the Chronicler shows his ideal king, David, as acting not on his own, but in consultation with his ministers and by involving the people in his decisions. An ironic reader might call him 'a virtual democrat'. This feature is not confined to this particular passage, but recurs in other scenes in the book that reflect the principle of persuasion and a near-democratic image of a nation in charge of its destiny.[15] We might note in passing that underlying the 'democratic' description lies

15. Here are some more examples showing that the monarch in Chronicles con-sults not only his ministers, but—what is more impressive—his people: 2 Chron. 14.6; 20.21; 25.17; 30.2, 4; 32.3.

the Chronicler's belief that God governs the world by a principle of immediate and personal retribution: the sinner is the one punished. The Chronicler is therefore obliged, when it comes to national events, to emphasize the participation and responsibility of every individual in the decisions, and hence in the consequences.[16]

The congregation of Israel, whom David addresses in this passage, comprises all that are left in 'all the lands of Israel'.[17] It appears that the Chronicler is not satisfied with the usual phrase 'Land of Israel', but substitutes it into an innovative and unique term, 'Lands of Israel', presumably referring to the inheritances of the tribes, while creating an image of a broad land comprising many countries—almost suggestive of a federation of states. How large this land is may be learned from the boundaries given at the end of the passage, 'from Shihor of Egypt to Lebo-hamath'. 'All Israel' from 'all the lands of Israel', then, lived between 'Shihor of Egypt', which means the Nile,[18] and 'Lebo-hamath', which lies beyond Damascus in the north.[19] There can be no doubt that these boundaries represent an exegetical reference to the boundaries defined in Josh. 13.2-5, namely the land remaining to be conquered, and are the Chronicler's way of drawing attention to the expanses of the lands that were populated by the Israelites even before David's wars. Thus the Promised Land is shown as a historical reality.

The book of Chronicles also opens with a detailed description showing that the entire people of Israel, from far and wide, including 'the remaining kinsmen' and the priest and the Levites from their towns, participated in this event. Yet the book of Samuel, describing the same event—bringing the ark to Jerusalem—notes that: 'David and all the troops that were with him set out from Baalim to Judah to bring up

16. The question of reward and punishment will be discussed briefly below. A detailed discussion may be found in Japhet, *Ideology*, pp. 165-76.

17. Though the JPS Bible uses the phrase 'the territories of Israel', I prefer the literal translation in this case, because it reflects the Chronicler's perception of Israel as a great land, composed of many lands.

18. See Isa. 23.3 and Jer. 2.18. The mentioning of 'Shihor, which is close to Egypt' in Josh. 13.3 refers to the eastern branch of the Nile delta. See J. Gray, *Joshua, Judges, Ruth* (NCBC; Grand Rapids: Eerdmans; Basingstoke: Marshall, Morgan & Scott, 1986), p. 125.

19. 'Lebo-hamath', which may be understood as the entrance to Hamath, is mentioned many times throughout the Hebrew Bible, but mostly not in association with Shihor. As, e.g., see: Num. 13.21; Judg. 3.3; 2 Kgs 14.25; Amos 6.14; Ezek. 48.1.

from there the Ark of God…'(2 Sam. 6.2).[20] The image of the people of Israel acting in union, as a single entity called 'all Israel' is central to the book of Chronicles.[21]

The desire to glorify David and all his deeds underlies this account, which implies that the need to consult the Ark did not arise in the reign of Saul, but was prompted entirely by David's initiative. [22]

This short, idealized picture was part of a larger concept, in which not only was the land of Israel spacious, but also it was densely inhabited. The Chronicler has a singular demographic outlook, with annexationist tendencies, to exaggerate the size of the nation. Here are two examples. In describing Solomon's building projects, the Chronicler refers to the numbers of the labourers mentioned in the book of Kings: '70,000 porters and 80,000 quarriers in the hills' (1 Kgs 5.29), who were given in bond service out 'of the Amorites, Hittites, Perizzites, Hivites and Jebusites, who were not of the Israelite stock (1 Kgs 9.20). In the book of Chronicles, all these are strangers in the land: 'Solomon took a census of all the aliens who were in the land of Israel…He made 70,000 of them basket carriers and 80,000 of them quarriers' (2 Chron. 2.16-17).[23] Thus the Gentile population, though Canaanite but labelled 'aliens', becomes attached to Israel as an inseparable part of the nation,

---

20. Though later on the text of Samuel has 'all the House of Israel' (2 Sam. 6.5), since it is not a case of organized gathering it would appear that it refers to the people who were with him and those who came along.

21. Japhet, *Ideology*, pp. 270-78.

22. The anti-Saulic tendency is also typical to Chronicles and it is emphasized in the description of Saul's death (1 Chron. 10) and especially in its ending (vv. 13-14). For a detailed analysis of this story, in comparison to the one in the book of Samuel, see in my article: 'Three Variations on the Death of Saul: Studies in the Fashioning of the World, in Reliability and in the Tendentiousness of Biblical Narrative' (Heb.), *Beth Mikra* 100.1 (1985), pp. 92-102.

23. In using the term 'aliens' (MT: *gērim*) the Chronicler ignores the direct connection between the people from the 'seven nations' and the labourers. According to him, those who live in the land of Israel are attached to the people of Israel, and may even participate in the cult, as for example, in the Passover rite (2 Chron. 30.25). He seems to base the legality of this on P (Exod. 12.48-49). In this context it is worth noting 2 Chron. 2.1, which strengthens the connection with 1 Kgs 5.29, thus making it clear that the author meant the same 150,000 people. On this interpretation, see Japhet, *Ideology*, pp. 334-51.

much like the multitude which accompanied the Israelites in their exodus from Egypt. This reveals the significance of the nation's size in the view of the Chronicler.

This tendency of depicting a vast and united people is especially marked in his treatment of the northern population. According to the Chronicler, the tribes of Ephraim and Manasseh were invited by Hezekiah to the first Passover he celebrated after the defeat and exile of the northern kingdom.[24] But because of the circumstances, the Passover was held only in the second month, after the priests had purified themselves and after the king had consulted his officers and the people and had issued a proclamation:

> ... throughout all Israel from Beer-Sheba to Dan that they come and keep the Passover for the Lord God of Israel in Jerusalem . . . As the couriers passed from town to town in the land of Ephraim and Manasseh till they reached Zebulun, they were laughed at and mocked. Some of the people of Asher and Manasseh and Zebulun, however, were contrite, and came to Jerusalem (2 Chron. 30.5-11).

This is a very different picture from the one given in the books of Kings and Ezra. These books describe the northern part of the country as emptied of its Israeli inhabitants by the Assyrian conquerors, then resettled with an imported foreign population.[25] And indeed, it is generally thought that the Assyrian policy of transferring populations of various sizes was a method of controlling the empire.[26] Yet the Chronicler describes the continuing presence of the original Israelite population as still belonging to the familiar tribes, not being influenced by the exile but being influenced by the kings of Judah. Josiah's reform, too, which took place after the northern expulsion, is described by the Chronicler as embracing the entire land of Israel, including 'the towns of Manasseh and Ephraim and Simeon, as far as Naphtali' (2 Chron. 34.6). Here it is interesting to note that he plays down the extent and significance of the deportation of northern Israel, referring to it only in the genealogical lists at the opening chapters of the book,[27] and there too as affecting only the two and a half tribes on the east bank of the Jordan (1 Chron. 5.25-26).

24. On the dimensions of the northern exile see in what follows.
25. See 2 Kgs 17.6, 24-41; 18.11-12; Ezra 4.1-2, 9-10.
26. See above Chapter 2 n. 15.
27. The opening chapters, which function as an exposition to the whole book, are 1 Chron. 1–9.

For Japhet, the analysis of all the changes and innovations of the Chronicler in relation to his sources led to the following conclusions: 'The inhabitants of Samaria were, along with the "resident aliens", descendants of Israelite tribes, the Judeans' brothers and an organic part of the people of Israel'.[28] 'Chronicles presents a different view of history: the dimensions of the Babylonian conquest and exile are reduced considerably, the people's settlement in the land is portrayed as an uninterrupted continuum.'[29] We may therefore conclude that as far as the Chronicler is concerned, the proper subject-matter is the great nation of Israel in the great land of Israel, and its continuous habitation therein.

A brief picture of the way of life in Israel during the First Temple period, as depicted in the book of Chronicles, has the temple in Jerusalem at its epicentre. That is why transferring the ark to Jerusalem is described as David's first act after he became king. The Chronicler also provides a detailed description of the extensive preparations David made towards the dedication of the temple (1 Chron. 22–29). The construction and dedication of the temple similarly occupies centre stage in the account of Solomon's acts, and as we have seen the occasion being invested with the magnitude of the Mount Sinai event, namely, as a ceremonious covenant between God and his people. Needless to say, the Chronicler ascribes the greatest importance to the celebrations and purifications which took place at the temple, and his book concludes with the reconstruction of the temple following the proclamation of Cyrus.

In contrast to its sources, in which the prophets play a central role in running the life of the people, and where the kings are shown warts and all, the book of Chronicles describes the kingdom of the house of David as the kingdom of God. The rule of the Davidic House over Israel embodies the kingdom of God, while the priests and prophets are left in the shadow of the king, who is God's single, personal representative.[30]

God is depicted in the book of Chronicles as the one and only deity who governs history, according to the strict theory of direct and immediate retribution. A historical narrative that seeks to demonstrate such a theory in action must often resort to divine intervention, either to

28. Japhet, *Ideology*, p. 334.

29. Japhet, *Ideology*, p. 386.

30. On this subject, see my article: 'The Role of Prophets and Prophecy in the Teachings of Chronicles' (Heb.), *Beth Mikra* 93.2 (1983), pp. 113-33.

reward or to punish. That is why Chronicles is especially rife with miracles and providential revelations, and God is not kept behind the scenes
in its historical account.

The attempt to fathom this extraordinary account leads me to two
conclusions regarding the book of Chronicles as a historiographical
work.

1. The purpose of the work was not purely historiographic. The
    author did not mean to record the past, or to complete the
    accounts which he found in his sources. Indeed, he had no
    intention of providing a thorough and extensive historical
    description. The Chronicler's selective use of his sources
    testifies to the book's tendentious purpose, which uses history
    merely as the groundwork on which to present his ideas.
    Nevertheless, the fact that the book was written as a histori-
    ography means that we can only discern the author's philos-
    ophy indirectly.

2. The second conclusion has to do with a more precise
    definition of the book's intention. The view that is accepted by
    some scholars is that the book reflects the time of its composi-
    tion, the contemporary ideological struggle with past concepts,
    and the need to adapt and rework them to the demands of the
    present and future. In other words, the book expresses the
    spiritual needs of the society in which it was written. There-
    fore its significance must not be reduced to an abstract ideo-
    logical contention; it must also be read as a polemical work,
    expressing a position in a concrete political-cultural debate, in
    which the author refers to immediate issues such as the atti-
    tude towards the population in the province of Samaria,
    towards foreigners and towards the temple rituals. In addition,
    the book expresses actual political ambitions, such as the
    restoration of the Davidic monarchy. The book must therefore
    be regarded as the expression of the social-political aims of
    an intellectual group that lived in the Second Temple period,
    towards the end of the Persian period, and which disagreed
    with the official line that we know from the books of Ezra
    and Nehemiah, the line that came to represent post-biblical
    Judaism. In contrast to the books of Ezra and Nehemiah,
    which, like Deuteronomy, approved of the separation from
    strangers—dubbed 'the adversaries of Judah and Benjamin'

(Ezra 4.1), as well as 'the peoples of the land' (Ezra 9.11); in contrast to those books, which described the removal of alien elements from the religious worship in Jerusalem and the expulsion of the foreign wives, Chronicles recommends welcoming strangers and making them into sojourners, as well as accepting mixed marriages—in brief, it expresses the kind of openness which may be found in the first four books of the Pentateuch and in the book of Ruth. The Chronicler is evidently referring to his own time, and using his historiographic work to express his ideological stance towards the 'Samaritan problem',[31] and towards the integration of strangers into the population of the Judaean districts, which considered itself to be of 'the holy seed' (Ezra 9.2). In the same way, his description of the House of David, and the emphasis on the role of the Levites in the ritual, was a way of protesting against the corrupt rule of the priests in his time. It should be noted that disillusion with the priesthood, combined with support for the expulsion of foreign wives, may be found in the prophecy of Malachi, who was probably a contemporary of Nehemiah.[32]

We may conclude by stating that the book of Chronicles is not an eschatological work. It expresses a complex criticism, at times direct and at others subtle and indirect, regarding the prevailing situation in its time, and proposes solutions which the author believes to be realistic, since they consist of returning to the conditions of the First Temple period. To do this, he uses his sources but adapts them as required. He does not copy mechanically, though he frequently quotes both the Pentateuchal and prophetic literature (the Former Prophets and the Latter Prophets). His quotes are part of his ideological contention with the preceding literature, that is to say, of the polemic he conducts by means of his sources.

It is not surprising that the exegetical tradition tended to ignore this book.[33] Throughout the centuries the exegetes could not cope with its

31. The northern population, who are of the province of Samaria, who would later be called Samaritans.

32. J.M.P. Smith, *The Book of Malachi* (ICC; Edinburgh: T. & T. Clark, 1961 [1912]), p. 8.

33. See E.L. Curtis and A.L. Madsen, *The Books of Chronicles* (ICC; New York: Charles Scribner's Sons, 1910), pp. 44-48: 'The Books of Chronicles...have never been a favorite field of study and investigation, hence their literature has

alterations and contradictions. But to us, the biblical researchers, this book is a unique treasure trove. It teaches us about the writing methods of the biblical authors, and the licence they took to express their views.

The next chapter, which in some way responds to the discussion about the book of Chronicles, will revolve around the issue of credibility and ideology—in other words, is a predominantly ideological account worthless as history?

always been relatively meagre' (the citation is taken from p. 44). See also Willi, *Die Chronik*, pp. 12-47.

Chapter 10

IDEOLOGICAL WRITING AS A HISTORICAL SOURCE

The last chapter which dealt with Chronicles highlighted the problem of the relationship between ideology and historical credibility; or, to put it another way, the extent to which a history written from an ideological viewpoint allows for a credible account, and of what value it may be. The various instances taken from the book of Chronicles might support the assumption that when ideology holds centre stage and history is used as its prop or as a means to an end, it is doubtful that a credible historical account may result. To nineteenth-century scholars, such as the above-mentioned de Wette (1806),[1] Wellhausen (1878)[2] and others,[3] the book's obvious tendentiousness, and the fact that it was written long after the events it described, meant that it was entirely unreliable. That is why for many years commentators and researchers preferred to rely for historical credibility on the accounts in the books of Samuel and Kings, rather than on the book of Chronicles, and the latter was simply ignored. Already Spinoza, who lived in the seventeenth century, in his book *Tractatus Theologico-Politicus*, which deals with the various books of the Bible wrote:

> Of the two books of Chronicles I have nothing particular or important to remark, except that they were written some considerable time after Ezra, and perhaps after the restoration of the temple by Judas Maccabee...As

1. W.M.L. de Wette, *Beiträge zur Einleitung in das Alte Testament* (Darmstadt: Wissenschaftliche Buchgesellschaft, 1971 [1806–1807]).
2. Wellhausen, *Prolegomena*, pp. 171-227.
3. I confine myself to the decisive phrasing of C.C. Torrey (*The Composition and Historical Value of Ezra–Nehemiah* [BZAW, 2; Giessen: Ricker, 1896], p. 52): 'No fact of OT criticism is more firmly established than this; that the Chronicler, as a historian, is thoroughly untrustworthy. He distorts facts deliberately and habitually; invents chapter after chapter with the greatest freedom; and what is most dangerous of all, his history is not written for its own sake, but in the interest of an extremely one-sided theory'.

to the authorship of these books, their authority, usefulness and doctrine, I can say nothing. Indeed, I find it quite astonishing that they were accepted among the Sacred Books by those who excluded from the canon the book of Wisdom, the book of Tobit, and other books that are called known as the Apocryphal. But it is not my purpose to disparage the authority of the Chronicles; since they have been given universal acceptance, I also leave them, for what they are.[4]

The general disregard for the book seems to stem from its being considered unreliable and its contents untrustworthy.

In the previous chapter I noted that the Chronicler's historical description adheres to the strict doctrine of direct and immediate retribution. That is why he had to create a correlation between the events and the retribution that promptly followed. If a certain king sinned, he had to be punished in his own lifetime, and not his son's; and vice versa, if he behaved virtuously, he had to be rewarded directly. For example, Manasseh, who sinned and led others to sin, reigned for 55 years (698–642 BCE); and yet, according to the book of Kings, there were no national catastrophes during his reign. But the author of the book of Kings, though also a believer in reward and punishment, did not stick to the principle of immediate and direct retribution, and was not therefore obliged to describe Manasseh's punishment for all his sins, being evidently unimpressed by the fact that this sinner enjoyed a long life and an especially long reign. According to his philosophy, Manasseh's sins sealed the fate of Jerusalem and caused its destruction at the hands of the Babylonians in the reign of Zedekiah, which is decades later (586 BCE). Indeed, this account suited the author of the book of Kings, as it could explain why Josiah's piety and virtuous deeds failed to prevent the downfall. The book of Kings is flexible and untroubled by the time gap between the sins of the fathers and the punishment of the sons, as stated in the Ten Commandments: 'for I the Lord your God am an impassioned God, visiting the guilt of the parents upon the children, upon the third and upon the fourth generations of those who reject Me...' (Exod. 20.5; Deut. 5.9; and elsewhere).

Both Jeremiah and, even more emphatically, Ezekiel criticized that concept of retribution, preferring the direct and immediate one: 'What do you mean by quoting this proverb upon the soil of Israel, "Parents

---

4.   Baruch Spinoza, *Tractatus Theologico-Politicus* (trans. S. Shirley; Leiden: E.J. Brill, 1989 [Gebhardt edition, 1925]), p. 186.

eat sour grapes and their children's teeth are blunted?" As I live—declares the Lord GOD—this proverb shall no longer be current among you in Israel...The person who sins, only he shall die' (Ezek. 18.2-4; see also Jer. 31.29-30). The Chronicler supports Ezekiel's retributive principle, which was intended to induce the people to obey the religious statutes by promising immediate reward. He therefore emphasizes the reward that Manasseh received—namely, his long life and reign—and it is not surprising that he depicts Manasseh as a repentant. The Chronicler therefore tells the story of Manasseh being exiled as punishment for his sins, followed by his submission and entreaty to God, to which God responds and brings him back to his kingdom in Jerusalem. The resulting picture shows Manasseh as a penitent, who cleared the idolatrous elements from the Temple Mount, called on Judah to serve the Lord God of Israel, and even strengthened and fortified Jerusalem (2 Chron. 33.12-19). Thus, according to the book of Chronicles, the destruction of Jerusalem and Judah were not the outcome of Manasseh's sins, but of Zedekiah and his contemporaries, the Chronicler's history being inspired by the principle of immediate retribution rather than cumulative sin. The Chronicler's description of Manasseh's exile and his return to Jerusalem has given rise to arguments among scholars. Some maintain that the Chronicler made it up in order to support his ideology of retribution while others argue that there must be a historical element in it, since it is unlikely that the Chronicler would have made up a purely imaginary story with no basis in fact.[5] It should be noted that the Assyrian sources make no mention of the revolt of Manasseh or his deportation. On the contrary, Manasseh is mentioned as loyal to the Assyrian kings Esarhaddon and Assurbanipal, in whose times he reigned. Moreover, in view of Judah's political and economic hardships during Manasseh's reign, and the might of Assyria under Esarhaddon and Assurbanipal, it is unlikely that he would have dared to rebel. It would seem, then, that in the case of Manasseh, the Chronicler saw fit to create a historical exegesis, which may be qualified as a midrashic or aggadic interpretation, to support his ideology.[6]

5.　See Japhet, *Chronicles*, pp. 1002-1004.

6.　This conclusion is also supported by the structure of the chapter, that prefers the chiastic order rather than the historical one, and also rests on the close connection between Ahab and Manasseh. It appears that the Chronicler took the motif of repentance from the story of Naboth (1 Kgs 21.27-29).

Regarding King Hezekiah, about whose righteous acts the book of
Kings has little to say (devoting only two verses to his reform [2 Kgs
18.4, 22]), Chronicles devotes three whole chapters (2 Chron. 29–31),
which are entirely concerned with the reform and its results. The Chronicler was faced with a conundrum: why was Hezekiah punished with
the Assyrian invasion, if he carried out a reform and did what was right
in the eyes of the Lord? How was it possible that the righteous Hezekiah was punished with the siege of Sennacherib? Significantly, after
describing the reform, he introduces the Sennacherib episode in the
following words: 'After these faithful deeds, King Sennacherib of
Assyria invaded Judah and encamped against its fortified towns with
the aim of taking them over' (2 Chron. 32.1). The Chronicler needed to
imply that all the positive things he had written about the reform were
faithful,[7] and to emphasize that Sennacherib only thought he could
conquer the fortified cities of Judah. Nevertheless, he had to explain the
failure of the doctrine of retribution, how despite Hezekiah's wonderful
reform Sennacherib invaded Judah.[8] So he opens his account of the
invasion with a strong hint that the Assyrian king's plan would not suc-
ceed, thereby turning Sennacherib's campaign into a lost cause and
a devastating defeat. And so, according to the Chronicler, Sennacherib
did not actually seize the Judaean cities but only imagined that he
would be able to do so. In the meantime, Hezekiah consulted with his
ministers and his mighty men, prepared Jerusalem for the siege, built
up the broken city wall, stopped up the waters of the fountains outside
the city, and encouraged his people with these words: '"Be strong and
of good courage, do not be frightened or dismayed by the king of
Assyria or by the horde that is with him, for we have more with us than
he has with him. With him is an arm of flesh, but with us is the Lord
our God, to help us and to fight our battles". The people were encouraged by the speech of King Hezekiah of Judah' (2 Chron. 32.7-8).
Preparations which would take years to carry out were completed,

---

7.   Most commentators interpret the word *wehā'emet* as 'faithful', linking it
with the conclusion of 2 Chron. 31.20: 'He acted in a way that was good, upright,
and faithful'. However, it seems to me that the choice of a word that also means
'truth' (see, e.g., Jer. 42.5; Deut. 13.15) is not fortuitous, and suggests that the
Chronicler was aware of his own method of employing his sources and needed to
affirm their veracity.
8.   The Chronicler had two earlier accounts of this event: 2 Kgs 18–19 and Isa.
36–37.

according to the Chronicler, while Sennacherib was in Judah planning to conquer. In his account of Hezekiah's reign the impossible becomes possible, only because the king and his people trusted in God. Thus, Sennacherib's invasion becomes in the book of Chronicles another opportunity for describing the virtuousness of Hezekiah and for propounding the doctrine of retribution, that meant that Sennacherib never had a chance of winning. By contrast, the author of the book of Kings admits that Hezekiah surrendered to Sennacherib after the latter had conquered all the fortified cities of Judah, and paid him a heavy tribute (2 Kgs 18.13-16). It should be noted that the description in the book of Kings is supported by external evidence, such as the Sennacherib inscriptions and the frieze of the siege of Lachish from Nineveh, and the findings of archaeology at Lachish and other places.[9]

These examples of the Chronicler's attempts to make history conform to an ideological tenet—unlike the flexible approach in the book of Kings, where it is possible for Manasseh to sin yet go unpunished, and for Hezekiah to be righteous and yet be punished—reveal why many researchers have regarded the book of Chronicles as entirely unreliable, and the book of Kings as highly reliable. But this is to overlook the fact that the book of Kings, which expresses the Deuteronomistic world-view, is also subject to an ideology, and may also contain accounts of doubtful historicity, that might have been inserted with an ideological aim in mind. Two examples out of many will illustrate this point: the first is the story of the vineyard of Naboth the Jezreelite, as described in 1 Kings 21, while the subsequent reference to the affair in 2 Kgs 9.25-26 suggests rather different circumstances.[10] It seems that the version given in 1 Kings 21 was intended to convey the idea that the king was responsible for what went on in his country.[11] The second example is the description of Samaria being emptied of its

9.   See M. Cogan and H. Tadmor, *II Kings* (AB, 11; Garden City, NY: Doubleday, 1988), pp. 228-52.

10.   A. Rofé, 'The Vineyard of Naboth: The Origin and Message of the Story', *VT* 38.1 (1988), pp. 89-104.

11.   Y. Zakovitch, 'The Tale of Naboth's Vineyard—I Kings 21', Addendum in M. Weiss, *The Bible from Within: The Method of Total Interpretation* (Jerusalem: The Magnes Press, 1984), pp. 379-405. Obviously, the king's responsibility was a major issue in the Deuteronomistic school.

inhabitants as a result of the Assyrian deportations (2 Kgs 17.5, 23, 24-41; 18.11-12).[12] However, an inscription of the Assyrian king Sargon states that he exiled 27,290 inhabitants.[13] This would mean that many of the inhabitants of northern Israel were not sent into exile, and that the account in the book of Kings was designed to depict the northern inhabitants as alien people from whom the Judaeans ought to keep apart.

On the other hand, even in the book of Chronicles there are some credible details drawn by the author from other sources than those known to us. The discovery of the Siloam Inscription and the Hezekiah Tunnel confirmed the Chronicler's account that Hezekiah 'stopped up the spring of water of Upper Gihon, leading it downward west of the City of David' (2 Chron. 32.30).[14] Similarly, surveys and excavations in Judaea and the Negev have shown that in the eighth century BCE there was considerable development in urbanization and agricultural settlement in all parts of Judah, supporting the description in the book of Chronicles of the development of the kingdom in the reign of Uzziah (2 Chron. 26.3-15).[15]

In other words, we should distinguish between studying biblical historiography as a historical source and examining it as an ideological sermon, and avoid general statements and assumptions with regard to any of the books. The book of Chronicles is not necessarily pure ideology, just as the book of Kings is not necessarily a reliable historical account. Both these books, like the entire biblical historiography, reflect ideologies yet also contain credible historical data. The tendency to view Chronicles as mere ideology and the book of Kings as a reliable history is the outcome of the kind of ideology expressed by their

12. See also the beginning of the process in 2 Kgs 15.29 and its continuation in Ezra 4.1, 10.

13. *ANET*, pp. 284-85. See also Cogan and Tadmor, *Kings*, p. 200, who note that 'one should consider that areas outside of the capital were also depopulated', and they do not refer to the population of the whole country. In this context it is also interesting to follow other historical problems, via their interpretation, pp. 197-201.

14. Cf. 2 Chron. 32.3-5; 2 Kgs 20.20; Isa. 22.9-11. For the archaeological data see Y. Shiloh, 'Jerusalem', in E. Stern (ed.), *The New Encyclopaedia of Archaeological Excavations in the Holy Land*, II (Jerusalem: Israel Exploration Society and Carta, 1993), pp. 709-12.

15. H. Tadmor, 'Azriyau of Yaudi', *Scripta Hierosolymitana* 8 (1961), pp. 232-71.

respective authors. The concept of flexible retribution, by which the third and fourth generation may be punished for the sins of their forefathers, enabled the author—in this case, of the book of Kings—to adapt his ideology to the historical chain of events. By contrast, the principle of rigid and immediate retribution required that the author adapt history to his ideology. That is why the first impression made by the Chronicler's account is that it consists entirely of ideology. However, historical and archaeological research show that every account must be separately examined. The decision about the historical validity or ideological quality of each text must be obtained by a variety of research tools, as Nadav Na'aman put it:

> There are no shortcuts in the study of the book of Chronicles as an historical source. Each and every passage must be stringently examined by means of all the instruments of research at our disposal, while avoiding preconceived ideas regarding its historical reliability. Only this kind of comprehensive and critical discussion could lead to an appropriate use of this book as a source for the study of the history of Israel during the First Temple period, and such a systematic investigation may lead to a better appreciation of the various sources which the author of the book of Chronicles drew on in writing his composition.[16]

Having reiterated the role of ideology at the expense of history and its veracity, I feel that I have sinned against the subject and will try to atone for it. The discussion about historical reliability revolved around the narrated world, which is the account of the historical past, rather than the world of the narrator or author and his time and place, whether of the Chronicler or the author of any other book of biblical historiography. I should now like to turn the discussion away from the account in the book of Chronicles and the question of its credibility, to the author himself. I ought to emphasize again that I chose Chronicles out of many other possibilities precisely because so many scholars and commentators have cast doubt on its reliability. Yet, I would argue that to us, the late readers, this book is also a historical source as it reflects the time of its writing. While it is not a historical source for reconstructing the earlier period, that of the First Temple, it is a historical source for its author's world, for a particular reality during the Second Temple period. As such, there is no doubt about its reliability—it reflects the world of beliefs and opinions in which it was composed,

16. N. Na'aman, 'Pastoral Nomads in the southwestern Periphery of the Kingdom of Judah in the 9th-8th Centuries BCE' (Heb.), *Zion* 52.3 (1987), pp. 261-78.

and is of immeasurable value in reconstructing the Jewish world during the Second Temple period.

In his essay 'Moses', Ahad-Ha'am distinguished between what he called archaeological and historical truths.[17] Archaeological truth, he said, is what we accept as a reliable historical source for reconstructing the past, whereas historical truth is the contribution made by a given work to our understanding of the forces that shape history. This is how he put it: 'Not every archaeological truth is also historical truth. Historical truth is that, and that alone, which reveals the forces that go to mould the social life of mankind. Every man who leaves a perceptible mark on that life, though he may be a purely imaginary figure, is a real historical; his existence is an historical truth'.[18]

In this view, the question whether there really was a man Moses, whose life and actions matched the account given in the Pentateuchal literature, is altogether secondary and marginal. What matters above all is the existence in history of this figure, which has been fixed in the minds of the people for untold generations, and whose influence on its national life has not ceased from antiquity to the present. As Ahad-Ha'am put it,

> For even if you succeeded in demonstrating conclusively that the man Moses never existed, or that he was not such a man as we supposed, you would not thereby detract one jot from the historical reality of the ideal Moses—the Moses, has been our leader not only for forty years in the wilderness of Sinai, but for thousands of years in all the wildernesses in which we have wandered since the Exodus.[19]

Applying these ideas to the books of Joshua or Chronicles, we might say that even if there was no conquest of the land, and even if the entire account in the book of Joshua is fictitious, there remains the historical existence of the idea of the conquest which, once it was born, accompanied the people in its exilic wanderings, and may even have played a part in the rise of Zionism. It was not only Joshua's contemporaries who 'took Canaan by storm', but all who adhered to the idea and eventually brought it off. The same thing may be said about the reliability of

17. Ahad Ha'am (='one of the people') is the pseudonym of Asher Hirsch Ginzberg (1856–1927), Hebrew essayist, philosopher and zionist leader.

18. A.H. Ginzberg, 'Moses', in L. Simon (trans.), *Selected Essays by Ahad Ha'am* (Philadelphia: Jewish Publication Society of America, 1948 [1912]), pp. 307-29 (307).

19. Ahad Ha'am, 'Moses', p. 309.

the book of Chronicles. Even if it is entirely a historical sermon and all its contents are doubtful, the fact remains that towards the end of the Persian period there was an ideological circle which opposed the official policy and dreamed political dreams about a greater land of Israel, ruled by a king from the House of David, and about a great nation of Israel, an open society which did not keep itself apart and willingly accepted those who wished to join it. In this way the book of Chronicles provides an important insight into the universalist currents in the society of the Second Temple period.

In other words, even those historiographical works which are of doubtful reliability may be of great importance in illuminating the period in which they were written and helping to reconstruct it. Through them we may gain a better understanding of the social and cultural forces that operated in the society that gave birth and shaped these works. Chronicles or the book of Joshua, or any other book of doubtful value in terms of its historical account, is of great value in helping to understand the culture of the people of Israel and the ideological currents that ran through it.

In summary, we may conclude that since ideology is itself a part of history, the distinction between history and ideology is important when we choose which side of history we wish to examine—that which is described or that which does the describing.

Afterword

HISTORY, IDEOLOGY AND NARRATIVE ART

Until now the discussion turned on biblical historiography as a historical composition subordinated to ideologies that changed with the circumstances. The emphasis was on the time of writing each work, and on the ideology that guided its author. I shall devote the conclusion of this study to the appeal of this historiography, whose power of persuasion affected untold generations of readers, who read and re-read the history and adopted the ideology.

The historian, as opposed to a chronicler, is not content with recording past events in a disconnected fashion; he wishes also to tell a story that will interest the readers and induce them to go on reading. That is why historical writing resembles the art of fiction. The historian, much like the fiction writer, must consider narrative sequence, beginnings and endings, deeper meaning, characterization and the like—the same considerations that apply to the writing of literary fiction. The argument that history is not merely a science but also an art is often heard among scholars, and explains why some historians adopt the techniques of literature. The art of story-telling plays an important part in the interaction between writer and readers, and it is natural that historians who wish to influence, persuade and attract their readers find themselves, deliberately or not, employing literary methods.[1]

---

1.   For the past 100 years the relationship between history and fiction—or story-telling—has been extensively debated by historians and philosophers. Here are some examples: J.H. Hexter, *Reappraisals in History* (New York: Harper & Row, 1961); A. Marwick, *The Nature of History* (London: Macmillan, 1970); R. Barthes, 'Historical Discourse', in M. Lane (ed.), *Introduction to Structuralism* (trans. P. Wexler; New York: Basic Books, 1970), pp. 145-55; and the summarizing essay of H. White, 'The Historical Text as a Literary Artifact', *Clio* 3.3 (1974), pp. 277-303.

Once the connection between historical and literary writing was made, the newly developed tools of the science of literature and the willingness to examine the sacred biblical history as an aggregate of legends and folk-tales, helped to turn the attention to the poetics of biblical narrative, namely, to the literary art that served the biblical historiographers.

In his book *The Art of Biblical Narrative*, Robert Alter analysed the story of Ehud the son of Gera and his triumph over Moab (Judg. 3.12-30), and concluded: 'It is perhaps less historicized fiction than fictionalized history—history in which the feeling and the meaning of events are concretely realized through the technical resources of prose fiction'.[2]

Alter divides biblical fiction into two parts. The first part, containing the history of primaeval humanity, the stories of the patriarchs, the exodus from Egypt and the conquest of Canaan, he classifies as fiction in the guise of history. The second part, beginning with the Judges, is a history which has been given the characteristic, richly-imaginary, quality of fiction. In any case, 'The point is that fiction was the principal means which the biblical authors had at their disposal for realizing history'.[3] It is therefore legitimate to examine biblical historiography with the tools of the science of literature, to analyse the organization of the story and its style—namely, its vocabulary, syntactical structures and the literary forms it contains (e.g. songs, proverbs, prophecies); likewise, the viewpoint from which the story is told, whether by one of the protagonists or by the narrator; the narrative sequence of the story, the gaps in it, the way in which the characters are delineated, whether by

2. R. Alter, *The Art of Biblical Narrative* (New York: Basic Books, 1981), p. 41. In reaching this conclusion, Alter follows other scholars who pioneered the use of literary tools in biblical interpretation. I will mention only some of their main works: Gunkel, *Legends*; M. Buber, *Werke*. II. *Schriften zur Bibel* (Munich: Kösel Verlag, 1964); in English see N.N. Glatzer (ed.), *On the Bible: Eighteen Studies* (New York: Schocken Books, 1968); M. Weiss, *The Bible from Within: The Method of Total Interpretation* (Jerusalem: The Magnes Press, 1984 [Heb. 1962]); S. Bar-Efrat, *Narrative Art in the Bible* (Sheffield: Almond Press, 1989 [Heb. 1979]); M. Perry and M. Sternberg, The King through Ironic Eyes: The Narrator's Devices in Biblical Story of David and Bathsheba and Two Excursuses on the Theory of the Narrative Text' (Heb.), *HASIFRUT* 1.2 (1968), pp. 263-92; see also, M. Sternberg, *The Poetics of Biblical Narrative: Ideological Literature and the Drama of Reading* (Bloomington: Indiana University Press, 1987).

3. Alter, *Narrative*, p. 32.

their appearance, their discourse or their thoughts; in short—all the means by which a historical account that could easily be dull and tedious is turned into a gripping and significant tale. The biblical author invents monologues and dialogues for his characters which no court writer could have known. He knows what Tamar said to her brother Amnon before and after the rape; what Delilah said to Samson each time she tried to entice him; how Jezebel made Ahab's heart merry when he was lying on his bed heavy and displeased because Naboth would not sell him his vineyard. He knows not only what Saul thought or felt, but also what God himself thought, foresaw and planned. As Alter puts it:

> The author of the David stories stands in basically the same relation to Israelite history as Shakespeare stands to English history in his history plays. Shakespeare was obviously not free to have Henry V lose the battle of Agincourt, or to allow someone else to lead the English forces there, but, working from the hints of historical tradition, he could invent a kind of *Bildungsroman*…surround him with invented characters that would serve as foils, mirrors…create a language and a psychology… making out of the stuff of history a powerful projection of human possibility. That is essentially what the author of the David cycle does for David…a host of other characters.[4]

In his book Alter chose to analyse the story of Ehud, son of Gera, being a tale that cannot be described as complex in its characterization or subtle in its thematic development. He assumed that the story's historical verisimilitude was quite reasonable, that it was rooted in a credible report about a real act of political terrorism that happened in history. That makes it all the more interesting to find the story so rich in the art of literary story-telling with its selections and combinations, all that has to do with the narrative and the manner of its telling. Let me briefly recount the story: the people of Israel did evil in the sight of the Lord and were subjugated by Moab. They cried to God, who sent them a deliverer, by name of Ehud the son of Gera, a lefthanded man. Ehud made himself a two-edged dagger which he hid under his clothes. After offering the king of Moab the present he had brought him he reached the summer parlour and asked to be left alone with the king. The king sent his men out and Ehud told him he had a message from God for him, the king rose and Ehud stabbed him with his dagger, closed the door and escaped. The king's servants, seeing the door shut, waited

4.   Alter, *Narrative*, pp. 35-36.

outside. In the interval Ehud mustered his army and captured the fords of the Jordan. When the Moabites discovered the murder they tried to flee but were caught at the fords. None of them escaped and the land was at peace for 80 years.

Alter discusses a number of literary features in this story, among them the satirical quality of the tale, its being almost a slapstick play, with the obese king Eglon being felled by Ehud, a representative of the thin subject people, and likewise all the fat warriors of Moab's army (Judg. 3.29) who were defeated by Ehud's troops. Alter suggests that the author got the idea of depicting the king of Moab as a fattened calf ready for slaughter from his name Eglon (*'egel* meaning calf in Hebrew). He analyses Ehud's equivocal statements to the king, 'I have a secret message for you' (Judg. 3.19), or 'I have a message for you from God' (v. 20), as referring simultaneously to his mission and his dagger, creating a dramatic irony. The humour is underlined by the servants' mistaken belief that their stout king is taking his time on the chamberpot, and similar features which belong in fiction rather than in a historical account.[5]

But Alter did not attempt to tackle the story of Ehud with the tools of historical analysis. Had he done so, he would have realized that the story lacks an element that is essential for historical writing, namely, a locale. The reader has no way of knowing where these events took place, where Eglon, king of Moab, was sitting—was it in his capital Heshbon, or the city he conquered, the city of palm trees, which may or may not be Jericho? Was he on the eastern bank of the Jordan, near the fords facing Moab, or on the western side of the river? All attempts by historians and commentators to reconstruct the historical event using the data in the story have run into further difficulties and the necessity of filling its many gaps.[6]

The historian Josephus Flavius, for instance, in his book *Antiquities of the Jews*, felt that the story was unreasonable from a historical viewpoint, and took pains to add and fill in many of the missing details in

5.   More literary features and an analysis of their meaning (after all, the function of the biblical narrative was not entertainment!) may be found in my essay, 'The Story of Ehud', pp. 97-123.

6.   On the attempts to answer all these questions, and the conclusion that the gaps are deliberate and part of the story's poetics, designed to bring out its meaning, see Amit, 'The Story of Ehud', pp. 97-123; and Amit, *The Book of Judges*, pp. 171-98.

order to turn it into a reasonable and credible account.[7] According to
Josephus, Eglon was residing in Jericho, and was on friendly terms
with Ehud. The latter won the goodwill of the king's courtiers with his
gifts, and was free to come and go in the court. The assassination took
place in the middle of a hot day, while the king's guards were at their
dinner table, and the king was resting in a room that was pleasant in
summer. Moreover, the populace of Jericho cooperated with Ehud and
helped him to summon the people. Josephus clearly felt that the biblical
story lacked the details which would explain where the event took place
and how Ehud managed to enter the royal residence, how he found his
way to the summer parlour, why the king trusted him and received him
privately, and other details which the historian, who requires a reasonable account, cannot overlook.

What then is the nature of the story of Ehud, which the historian
balks at accepting as a reasonable account, and a literary scholar views
as history treated as fiction? As I see it, it is an ideological tale designed
to create the effect of a historical account, using a variety of artistic
devices to strengthen its ideological message.[8] It expresses the ideas of
the book of Judges, depicting God as guiding history with justice, and
the leader who operates in history as God's messenger.[9] That is why the
story actually opens with the assertion that 'because they [Israel] did
what was offensive to the Lord, the Lord let King Eglon of Moab prevail over Israel' (Judg. 3.12). This king, thinking in human terms and
unaware that he is an instrument in the hand of Providence, strengthens
his position by an alliance with the Ammonites and Amalekites (v. 13).
Only then did the Israelites cry out to the Lord and the Lord raised
them up a deliverer (v. 15). The narrator proceeds to describe Ehud's
stratagems in detail, giving the impression of a perfect human plan, yet
leaves out some central and essential information about its operation.
We do not know what Ehud went through as he entered the place, we
do not know if the king was there when the present was offered, or how
Ehud reached the summer parlour, which the king had for himself
alone. The effort to discover these details reveals too many well-timed

7.   Josephus, *Ant.* 5.185-97.
8.   I am indebted to my teacher Meir Sternberg for the understanding of biblical narrative as elaborated and so sophisticated literature.
9.   See above, Chapter 3.

coincidences, suggesting to the reader of biblical literature that Providence has taken a hand in the events to lead them to a successful conclusion.[10] The description of the stabbing of the king creates the same effect. Ehud used his lefthandedness as a ruse, and the king did not suspect him because he did not use his right hand, but thereafter things happen by themselves—he does not need to hide the murder weapon, because the fat closed upon the blade and the hilt: 'and the hilt went in after the blade' (v. 22). Similarly, a chance that he could hardly have foreseen enabled him to lock the door behind him, and so was the amazing timing after his exit: 'After he left, the courtiers returned' (v. 24); or 'But Ehud had made good his escape while they delayed (v. 26). Equally amazing is the statement that none of the Moabites escaped, though there has never been a battle in which not a single survivor remained on the defeated side. In other words, there are in the story of Ehud, son of Gera, both reasonable elements and coincidences which suggest the working of providence. The author demonstrates to his readers that the success of stratagems on the human level depends on divine providence, and may be achieved only through God's power and will. It is this divine intervention behind the scenes which assures the victory over Moab and the effectiveness of Ehud's plans. Man is depicted as an instrument in the historical scheme which God supervises and guides.

The story of Ehud was one example. The examination of other stories yields additional ideologies. For example, in the book of Joshua it is the harlot Rahab who is the mouthpiece of Deuteronomistic ideology.[11] She is depicted as an authority on history, able to expound on the Israelite exodus from Egypt and their triumph over the Amorites, whom they utterly destroyed; she acknowledges the superiority and exclusivity of their God, YHWH, and is therefore convinced that they are destined to conquer Jericho:

> She said to the men: 'I know that the Lord has given the country to you, because dread of you has fallen upon us, and all the inhabitants of the land are quaking before you. For we have heard how the Lord dried up the water of the Sea of Reeds for you when you left of Egypt, and what

10. On the direct connection between God and events, their timing and their significance as God's intervention, see, e.g., Gen. 24.11-27; the book of Jonah, with the repetition of the verb '[God] provided' (*way^{e}man*): 2.1; 4.6, 7, 8.

11. On the conquest of the land as part of the Deuteronomistic editing, see Chapter 7.

you did to Sihon and Og, the two Amorite kings across the Jordan, whom
you doomed. When we heard about it, we lost heart...for the Lord your
God is the only God in heaven above and on earth below' (Josh. 2.9-13).

The shaping of the plot and the characterization of the personae in
the story of the vineyard of Naboth the Jezreelite express an ideology
which sees the king as the central figure, and holds him responsible for
all that happens in his kingdom (1 Kgs 21).[12] Thus, although Ahab
is shown as passive while Jezebel takes the initiative—she gives the
order, writes the letters, seals them, sends them to the elders and the
nobles in Jezreel, tells them to proclaim a fast and set Naboth at the
head of the people, and sends two men to bear witness against him—
when Elijah brings the word of God, it is Ahab who is to be punished
and not Jezebel. Despite her meticulous plan to eliminate Naboth and
inherit his vineyard, God and the prophet address the king and accuse
him with the words: 'Would you murder and take possession?' (1 Kgs
21.19)—because the responsiblity lies with him. There are many more
examples that show that it is not enough to examine the history and the
ideology, it is also necessary to look at the art of story-telling.

Alter raised the question, 'are we not coercing the Bible into being
"literature" by attempting to transfer such categories to a set of texts
that are theologically motivated, historically oriented, and perhaps to
some extent collectively composed?'[13] The answer is that we are not.
Not only because today the connection between historical and literary
writing is widely recognized, but because the drive behind biblical historical writing is not the recording of history but ideological persuasion,
and whoever sets out to persuade must use rhetoric and the subtle,
direct or indirect, devices of the art of fiction.

In this study, which was devoted to history and ideology in biblical
literature, I noted first the importance of the history, and the ideological
motive behind this phenomenon. History served as the platform on
which to present a new and different religion, at the centre of which
stands a one and single God, creator of the world, who rules it in accordance with principles of justice and morality. The history came to
replace the myths and broad epics. At the same time, renouncing the
myths and epics did not mean renouncing their mode of expression,

12. See Chapter 10, n. 11.
13. Alter, *Narrative*, pp. 23-24.

namely, the poetics which shaped them. That is why the basis of biblical historiography appears in the form of stories.

To sum up: the art of story-telling plays an important part in the relation between history and ideology, that is, in conveying history as a narrative and in its manner of presentation. A story can reach a broader audience and arouse its interest, and clever depiction serves to deepen the ideological messages. It is not surprising that the biblical historiographers chose the story as their principal means of recounting history. Examining these stories from the viewpoint of literary art reveals that these writers, while reflecting their various ideological schools, were also master-craftsmen, able to turn history into an account which is often replete with fiction and always with literary devices, but is so organized as to reveal to the reader the meaning of history.

BIBLIOGRAPHY

Ahituv S., *Joshua: Introduction and Commentary* (Mikra Leyisra'el; Tel Aviv: Am Oved Publishers; Jerusalem: Magnes Press, 1995 [Heb.]).

Alt, A., 'The Settlement of the Israelites in Palestine', in *idem*, *Essays on Old Testament History and Religion* (trans. R.A. Wilson; Garden City, NY: Doubleday, 1966), pp. 175-221.

Alter, R., *The Art of Biblical Narrative* (New York: Basic Books, 1981).

Amit, Y., *The Book of Judges: The Art of Editing* (Jerusalem and Tel Aviv: The Bialik Institute, 1992 [Heb.]); ET trans. J. Chipman, Leiden: E.J. Brill, 1999.

—'The Position of the Exodus Tradition in the Book of Chronicles', in B. Uffenheimer (ed.), *Te'uda 2: Bible Studies Y.M. Grintz in Memoriam* (Heb.) (Tel Aviv: Hakibbutz Hameuchad Publishing House, 1982), pp. 139-55.

—'The Role of Prophets and Prophecy in the Teachings of Chronicles' (Heb.), *Beth Mikra* 93.2 (1983), pp. 113-33.

—'*The Story of Ehud* (Judges 3.12-30): The Form and the Message', in J.C. Exum (ed.), *Signs and Wonders: Biblical Texts in Literary Focus* (Semeia Studies; Atlanta: Scholars Press, 1989), pp. 97-123.

—'Teaching the Book of Joshua and its Problems' (Heb.), *Al Haperek* 2 (Jerusalem: The Ministry of Education and Culture, 1986), pp. 16-22.

—'Three Variations on the Death of Saul: Studies in the Fashioning of the World, in Reliability and in the Tendentiousness of Biblical Narrative' (Heb.), *Beth Mikra* 100.1 (1985), pp. 92-102.

Auerbach, E., 'Odysseus' Scar', in *idem*, *Mimesis: The Representation of Reality in Western Literature* (Princeton, NJ: Princeton University Press, 1953), pp. 3-23.

Bar-Efrat, S., *Narrative Art in the Bible* (Sheffield: Almond Press, 1989 [Heb. 1979]).

Barthes, R., 'Historical Discourse', in M. Lane (ed.), *Introduction to Structuralism* (trans. P. Wexler; New York: Basic Books, 1970), pp. 145-55.

Blenkinsopp, J., 'Are There Traces of the Gibeonite Covenant in Deuteronomy?', *CBQ* 28 (1966), pp. 207-13.

Buber, M., *Kingship of God* (trans. R. Scheimann; London: Allen & Unwin, 3rd edn, 1967).

—*Werke*. II. *Schriften zur Bibel* (Munich: Kösel Verlag, 1964).

Burney, C.F., *The Book of Judges* (New York: Ktav, 1970 [1903, 1918]).

Butterfield, H., 'Historiography', *Encyclopaedia Hebraica*, XIV (Jerusalem and Tel Aviv: Encyclopaedia Publishing Company, 1960; Heb.), pp. 259-318.

Carr, E.H., *What is History?* (Harmondsworth: Penguin Books, 1961).

Cassuto, U.M.D., 'The Rise of Historiography in Israel' (Heb.), *Eretz-Israel* 1 (1951), pp. 85-88; repr.; U.M.D. Cassuto, 'The Beginning of Historiography among the Israelites', in *idem*, *Biblical and Canaanite Literatures: Studies on the Bible and Ancient Orient*, I (Jerusalem: Magnes Press, 1972 [Heb.]), pp. 12-19.

Cogan M., and H. Tadmor, *II Kings* (AB, 11; Garden City, NY: Doubleday, 1988).

Collingwood, R.G., *The Idea of History* (Oxford: Oxford University Press, 1946).

Cross, F.M., *Canaanite Myth and Hebrew Epic* (Cambridge, MA: Harvard University Press, 1973).

Crüsemann, F., *Der Widerstand gegen das Königtum* (WMANT, 49; Neukirchen–Vluyn: Neukirchener Verlag, 1978).

Curtis, E.L., and A.L. Madsen, *The Books of Chronicles* (ICC; New York: Charles Scribner's Sons, 1910).

Davies, P.R., *In Search of 'Ancient Israel'* (JSOTSup, 148; Sheffield: JSOT Press, 1992).

Demsky, A., 'Literacy in Israel and among Neighboring Peoples in the Biblical Period' (Thesis submitted to the Hebrew University, Jerusalem 1976 [Heb.]).

Ehrlich, E.L., 'Der Aufenthalt des Königs Manasse in Babylon', *TZ* 21 (1965), pp. 281-86.

Eichrodt, W., *Theology of the Old Testament*, I (trans. J.A. Baker; Philadelphia: SCM Press, 1967).

Emerton, J.A., 'New Light on Israelite Religion: The Implications of the Inscriptions from Kuntillet 'Ajrud', *ZAW* 94.1 (1982), pp. 2-20.

Engnell, I., *Studies in Divine Kingship in the Ancient Near East* (Oxford: Basil Blackwell, 2nd edn, 1967).

Finkelstein, I., *The Archaeology of the Israelite Settlement* (Jerusalem: The Israel Exploration Society, 1988).

Frankfort, H., *Kingship and the Gods* (Chicago: University of Chicago Press, 1948).

Friedman, R.E., *Who Wrote the Bible* (New York: Summit Books, 1987).

Gadd, C.J., *Ideas of Divine Rule in the Ancient East* (London: Oxford University Press, 1943).

Garmonsway, G.N. (ed. and trans.), *The Anglo-Saxon Chronicle* (London and New York: J.M. Dent, 1972).

Geller, S.A., *Sacred Enigmas: Literary Religion in the Hebrew Bible* (London: Routledge, 1996).

Gerbrandt, G.E., *Kingship According to the Deuteronomistic History* (SBLDS, 87; Atlanta: University Microfilms International, 1986).

Ginzberg, A.H., 'Moses', in L. Simon (trans.), *Selected Essays by Ahad Ha'am* (Philadelphia: Jewish Publication Society of America, 1948 [1912]), pp. 307-329.

Glatzer, N.N. (ed.), *On the Bible: Eighteen Studies* (New York: Schocken Books, 1968).

Godley, A.D. (trans.), *Herodotus: In Four Volumes* (LCL; Cambridge, MA: Harvard University Press; London: Heinemann, 1946).

Gottwald, N.K., *The Tribes of Yahweh* (Maryknoll, NY Orbis Books, 1979).

Gray, J., *I & II Kings* (OTL; London: SCM Press, 3rd edn, 1977).

—*Joshua, Judges, Ruth* (NCBC; Grand Rapids: Eerdmans; Basingstoke: Marshall, Morgan & Scott, 1986).

Gunkel, H., *The Legends of Genesis: The Biblical Saga and History* (trans. W.H. Carruth; New York: Schocken Books, 1964).

Guttmann, J., *Philosophies of Judaism: The History of Jewish Philosophy from Biblical Times to Franz Rosenzweig* (trans. D.W. Silverman; New York, Chicago, San Francisco: Holt, Rinehart & Winston, 1964).

Hexter, J.H., *Reappraisals in History* (New York: Harper & Row, 1961).

Heym, S., *The King David Report* (New York: Putnam, 1973; German edn 1972).

Hoffmann, H.D., *Reform und Reformen: Untersuchungen zu einem Grundthema der deuteronomistischen Geschichtsschreibung* (ATANT, 66; Zürich: Theologischer Verlag, 1980).

Hyatt, J. P., *Exodus* (NCBC; Grand Rapids: Eerdmans, 1980).

Japhet, S., *I & II Chronicles* (OTL; Louisville, KY: Westminster/John Knox Press, 1993).

—*The Ideology of the Book of Chronicles and its Place in Biblical Thought* (trans. A. Barber; Frankfurt am Main: Peter Lang, 1989 [Heb. edn 1977]).

Kearney, P.J., 'The Role of the Gibeonites in the Deuteronomic History', *CBQ* 35 (1973), pp. 1-19.

Knohl, I., *The Sanctuary of Silence: The Priestly Torah and the Holiness School* (Minneapolis: Fortress Press, 1995).

Lemche, N.P., *Early Israel: Anthropological and Historical Studies on the Israelite Society before the Monarch* (VTSup, 37; Leiden: E.J. Brill, 1985).

Licht, J.S., 'Pleasing, Pleasing Odor', *Encyclopaedia Biblica*, V (Jerusalem: The Bialik Institute, 1968 [Heb.]), pp. 831-32.

Marwick, A., *The Nature of History* (London: Macmillan, 1970).

Mayes, A.D.H., 'Deuteronomy 4 and the Literary Criticism of Deuteronomy', *JBL* 100 (1981), pp. 23-51.

McKenzie, S.L., *The Trouble with Kings: The Composition of the Book of Kings in the Deuteronomistic History* (VTSup, 42; Leiden: E.J. Brill, 1991).

Mendenhall, G.E., 'The Hebrew Conquest of Palestine', *BA* 25 (1962), pp. 66-87.

Momigliano, A.D., *Studies in Historiography* (London: Weidenfeld & Nicolson, 1966).

Montgomery, J.A., *The Books of Kings* (ICC; New York: Charles Scribner's Sons, 1951).

Moore, G.F., *Judges* (ICC; Edinburgh: T. & T. Clark, 1966 [1895]).

Murphy, R.E., *Ecclesiastes* (WBC, 23A; Dallas: Word Books, 1992).

Na'aman, N., 'The "Conquest of Canaan" in Joshua and in History', in N. Na'aman and I. Finkelstein (eds.), *From Nomadism to Monarchy: Archaeological and Historical Aspects of Early Israel* (Jerusalem: Yad Izhak Ben-Zvi, The Israel Exploration Society, 1990 [Heb.]), pp. 284-347.

—'The Debated Historicity of Hezekiah's Reform in the Light of Historical and Archaeological Research', *ZAW* 107 (1995), pp. 179-95.

—'Historiography, the Fashioning of the Collective Memory, and the Establishment of Historical Consciousness in Israel in the Late Monarchial Period' (Heb.), *Zion* 60.4 (1995), pp. 449-72.

—'Pastoral Nomads in the Southwestern Periphery of the Kingdom of Judah in the 9th-8th Centuries BCE' (Heb.), *Zion* 52.3 (1987), pp. 261-78.

Nelson, R.D., *The Double Redaction of the Deuteronomistic History* (JSOTSup, 18; Sheffield: JSOT Press, 1981).

Noth, M., *Überlieferungsgeschichtliche Studien* (Tübingen: M. Niemeyer, 1943); ET *The Deuteronomistic History* (JSOTSup, 15; Sheffield: JSOT Press, 1981).

—*Exodus* (OTL; trans. J.S. Bowden; London: SCM Press, 2nd edn, 1966).

O'Connell, R.H., *The Rhetoric of the Book of Judges* (Leiden : E.J. Brill, 1996).

Oded, B., *Mass Deportation and Deportees in the Neo-Assyrian Empire* (Wisebaden: L. Reichert, 1979).

Perry, M., and M. Sternberg, 'The King through Ironic Eyes: The Narrator's Devices in Biblical Story of David and Bathsheba and Two Excursuses on the Theory of the Narrative Text' (Heb.), *HASIFRUT* 1.2 (1968), pp. 263-92.

Rad, G. von, 'The Beginnings of Historical Writing in Ancient Israel', in *The Problem of the Hexateuch and Other Essays* (trans. E.W. Trueman Dicken; Edinburgh: Oliver & Boyd, 1966), pp. 166-204.

— *Das Geschichtsbild des chronistischen Werkes* (Stuttgart: W. Kohlhammer, 1930).

—*Old Testament Theology*. I. *The Theology of Israel's Historical Traditions* (trans. D.M.G. Stalker; Edinburgh: Oliver & Boyd, 1962).

— *Studies in Deuteronomy* (SBT, 9; trans. D. Stalker, London: SCM Press, 1963).

Richter, W., *Die Bearbeitungen des 'Retterbuches' in der deuteronomischen Epoche* (BibB, 21; Bonn: P. Hanstein, 1964).

—*Traditionsgeschichtliche Untersuchungen zum Richterbuch* (BibB, 18; Bonn: P. Hanstein, 1963).

Rofé, A., 'The Monotheistic Argumentation in Deuteronomy IV 32-40: Contents, Composition and Text', *VT* 35 (1985), pp. 434-45.

— *The Prophetical Stories: The Narratives about the Prophets in the Hebrew Bible, their Literary Types and History* (Jerusalem: Magnes Press, 1986 [Heb.]).

—'The Vineyard of Naboth: The Origin and Message of the Story', *VT* 38.1 (1988), pp. 89-104.

Rothstein, J.W., and J. Hänel, *Kommentar zum ersten Buch der Chronik* (KAT, 18; Leipzig: A. Deichter, 1927).

Rudolph, W., *Chronikbücher* (HAT, 21; Tübingen: J.C.B. Mohr [Paul Siebeck], 1955).

Seeligmann, I.L., 'On the History and Nature of Prophecy in Israel' (Heb.), *Eretz-Israel* 3 (1954), pp. 125-32.

Shiloh, Y., 'Jerusalem', in E. Stern (ed.), *The New Encyclopaedia of Archaeological Excavations in the Holy Land*, II (Jerusalem: Israel Exploration Society and Carta, 1993), pp. 709-12.

Smith, C.F. (trans.), *Thucydides*. I. *History of the Peloponnesian War Books 1 and 2* (4 vols.; LCL; Cambridge, MA; Harvard University Press; London: Heinemann, 1923–28).

Smith, J.M.P., *The Book of Malachi* (ICC; Edinburgh: T. & T. Clark, 1961 [1912]).

Spinoza, B., *Tractatus Theologico-Politicus* (trans. S. Shirley; Leiden: E.J. Brill, 1989).

Sternberg, M., *The Poetics of Biblical Narrative: Ideological Literature and the Drama of Reading* (Bloomington: Indiana University Press, 1987).

Tadmor, H., 'Azriyau of Yaudi', *Scripta Hierosolymitana* 8 (1961), pp. 232-71.

Thackeray, H.St.J. (trans.), *Josephus*. IV. *Jewish Antiquities, Books 1–4* (9 vols.; LCL; Cambridge, MA: Harvard University Press; London: Heinemann, 1977); V. *Books 5–8* (Cambridge, MA: Harvard University Press; London: Heinemann, 1958); VI. *Books 9–11* (LCL; Cambridge, MA: Harvard University Press; London: Heinemann, 1958).

Thompson, R.J., *Moses and the Law in a Century of Criticism Since Graf* (VTSup, 19; Leiden: E.J. Brill, 1970).

Thompson, T.L., *The Historicity of the Patriarchal Narratives* (BZAW, 133; Berlin: W. de Gruyter, 1974).

—*Early History of the Israelite People: From the Written and Archaeological Sources* (Leiden: E.J. Brill, 1992).

—*The Origin Tradition of Ancient Israel* (Sheffield: JSOT Press, 1987).

Torrey, C.C., *The Composition and Historical Value of Ezra–Nehemiah* (BZAW, 2; Giessen: Ricker, 1896).

Toy, C.H., *The Book of Proverbs* (ICC; Edinburgh: T. & T. Clark, 1959 [1899]).

Urbach, E.A., 'When Did Prophecy Cease? (Heb.)', *Tarbiz* 17 (1946), pp. 1-11.

Van Seters, J., *Abraham in History and Tradition* (New Haven: Yale University Press, 1975).

—*In Search of History: Historiography in the Ancient World and the Origins of Biblical History* (New Haven: Yale University Press, 1983).

Walsh, W.H., *An Introduction to Philosophy of History* (London: Hutchinson, 3rd edn, 1967 [1951]).

Weinfeld, M., *Deuteronomy and the Deuteronomic School* (Oxford: Clarendon Press, 1972).

—*From Joshua to Josiah: Turning Points in the History of Israel from the Conquest of the Land until the Fall of Judah* (Jerusalem: Magnes Press, 1992 [Heb.]).

Weinryb, E., *Historical Thinking: Issues in Philosophy of History* (Tel-Aviv: Everyman's University Publishing House, 1987; Heb).

Weiss, M., *The Bible from Within: The Method of Total Interpretation* (Jerusalem: The Magnes Press, 1984).

Wellhausen, J., *Prolegomena to the History of Ancient Israel* (trans. J.S. Black and A. Menzies; New York: Meridian Books, 2nd edn, 1958 [1878]).

Wette, W.M.L. de, *Beiträge zur Einleitung in das Alte Testament* (Darmstadt: Wissenschaftliche Buchgesellschaft, 1971 [1806–1807]).

—'Dissertatio critico-exegetica qua Deuteronomium a prioribus Pentateuchi Libris diversum, alius cuiusdam recentioris auctioris opus esse monstratur; quam... auctoritate amplissimi philosophorum ordinis pro venia legendi AD XXVIII' (Jena, 1805).

White, H., 'The Historical Text as a Literary Artifact', *Clio* 3.3 (1974), pp. 277-303.

Whybray, N., *The Making of the Pentateuch* (JSOTSup, 53; Sheffield: Sheffield Academic Press, 1987).

Willi, T., *Die Chronik aus Auslegung* (FRLANT, 106; Göttingen: Vandenhoeck & Ruprecht, 1972).

Williamson, H.G.M., *1 and 2 Chronicles* (NCBC; Grand Rapids: Eerdmans; London Marshall, Morgan & Scott, 1987 [1982]).

Yerushalmi, Y.H., *Zakhor: Jewish History and Jewish Memory,* (Seattle: University of Washington Press, 1982).

Young, I., 'The Style of Gezer Calendar and some "Archaic Biblical Hebrew" Passages', *VT* 42 (1992), pp. 362-75.

Zakovitch, Y., *'Every High Official Has a Higher One Set Over Him': A Literary Analysis of II Kings 5* (Tel Aviv: Am oved Publishers, 1985 [Heb.]).

—'The Tale of Naboth's Vineyard—I Kings 21', addendum in M. Weiss, *The Bible from Within: The Method of Total Interpretation* (Jerusalem: Magnes Press, 1984), pp. 379-405.

INDEXES

INDEX OF REFERENCES

BIBLE

INDEX OF AUTHORS